Critically Thinking Physical Geography: A Solution Handbook

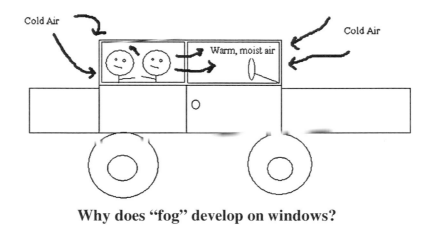

Why does "fog" develop on windows?

Ken Yanow

Critically Thinking Physical Geography: A Solution Handbook

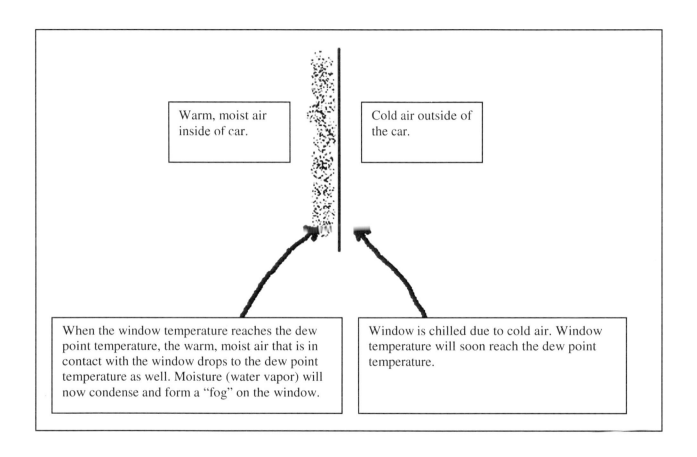

Warm, moist air inside of car.

Cold air outside of the car.

When the window temperature reaches the dew point temperature, the warm, moist air that is in contact with the window drops to the dew point temperature as well. Moisture (water vapor) will now condense and form a "fog" on the window.

Window is chilled due to cold air. Window temperature will soon reach the dew point temperature.

BookSurge Publications
ISBN: 1-4196-3342-2

For Samar, Sebastian, and Taran

Brief Contents

Contents

Contents

Contents

Contents

An Introduction to Critical Thinking

What is *critical thinking*? You've most likely heard this term before, but what exactly does it mean? Put simply, critical thinking is the ability to use what you know to solve what you need to know. Unfortunately, many students today are not taught the necessary tools to develop their critical thinking skills; skills for any class you take or any situation that requires thought.

As a college student, your typical goals are twofold (maybe more, but let's stick to two): 1) to pass your classes, and 2) to gain the necessary skills to be successful in your future endeavors (academic or otherwise). Typically, your success rate is dependent upon your ability to assimilate useful information and thoughtfully solve practical problems. The science of physical geography requires such skills. Contrary to popular belief, physical geography is more than geographic name memorization and place recognition. Rather it, like most physical science courses, requires you to solve dynamic, conceptual problems using strong critical thinking skills. A typical geography textbook, however, rarely devotes enough pages to the instruction of necessary problem solving. Regrettably, the results of skill-development-scarcity reflect itself in student outcomes. Students tend to do very well on factual exams, yet tend to do poorly when posed conceptual and critical thinking questions. Additional resources need to be made available. This book addresses those needs with a series of fully solved critical thinking questions covering challenging concepts typical in an introductory course. Ultimately, this book proves to be a step by step guide on *how* to solve problems.

The best way to use this book is as follows: 1) First, *understand* the question. Read it as many times as it takes until you understand what the question is asking. 2) *Think* about a solution. Don't just go straight to the solution in the book. Think first; look second. 3) Now, read the solution and do so multiple times. Make sure that you understand the solution and the steps it took to get to it. 4) Do the same procedure again before moving to the next question.

If you follow the aforementioned steps, it is expected that you will find greater success in your ability to grasp difficult concepts. In addition, it's expected that you will develop greater critical thinking skills and thereby become more adept at assimilating information to solve unique problems. This last expected outcome will not only help you succeed in physical geography, but aid you in your ultimate goal of being a successful, lifelong learner.

This supplemental textbook is designed for all students taking General Education (GE) Introductory Physical Geography coursework. It was written especially for the non-science major, but not exclusively for the non-science major. In addition, this supplemental textbook can be used with *any* Introductory Physical Geography textbook.

One last note: *Enjoy* your classes. Soon you'll be out in the 'real' world longing once again for the collegiate life. College classes (especially outside your major) might seem challenging, difficult, often times boring, and sometimes cumbersome; but ultimately the things you learn today across the entire spectrum of coursework, will make you who you are tomorrow.

Best Regards,
Ken Yanow
Professor of Geographical Sciences
Southwestern College

Tips for Success

Although each student is different, below are some helpful tips that will aid you in your successful completion in your classes (physical geography or otherwise).

❑ First of all, *attitude*: *nothing* is too difficult or out of your reach. *Never* say "I am not good in science," or, "I am not good in math," or, "I like the material but..." If you want to be successful, you first and foremost need to have a good attitude. I must stress, *do not* walk into any class with the attitude of "C, all I want is a C." If you do, you are setting yourself up to barely get by, which might not be good enough. You must have the attitude and aspiration to do your very best. Set high standards and high goals. Remember, you are in college; an institution of academic advancement to which you are *paying* to attend. You are here because you are ambitious. You want to learn. You want to succeed. Come to class prepared to do so.

❑ Ask questions in class, especially if you are confused. If you feel uncomfortable, ask questions during the faculty office hours or via email. Go to class daily. Do *all* of the homework assignments (and put time and effort into all of them).

❑ Time, time, time. You should not wait until the day before the exam to study for the exam. Learning is a constant task. You should set aside a minimum of 30 to 60 minutes per day to study the material -- reading the text, reviewing notes, answering study questions. 30 minutes is not a large amount of time. If you take the strategy of learning in small increments, you *will* learn and the class will be much more enjoyable. If you wait until the last minute to study, you will end up "cramming" the material (which will take you a few hours) and you will forget virtually everything after the exam (and, most likely, do mediocre on the exams...). So, where do you find the time? Create a daily schedule. You will have the time and you will see improvements immediately.

❑ Note taking: Be selective with your note taking. You need to find a way to listen to the instructor *and* take notes. Do not limit yourself to merely copying everything down that you see on the board or on the screen. If the instructor says something that sounds important to you, write it down. If the instructor uses full sentences on the board (and proper English), *don't* waste your time writing everything down verbatim. Use short hand notation that you understand. If you don't you will miss something that the instructor says. Here's a big tip: most instructors test the student on material that has been talked about in class. Listen as best you can (tape the lectures if possible), be selective and efficient with your note taking, and if anything confuses you ask questions. It's your class; you are paying for it, so don't worry about what other students think. Just worry about yourself.

❑ Daily, go home and *re-copy* your notes. If you don't you will almost certainly forget the material. It is a proven fact that students who re-copy their notes learn the material quicker, with greater comprehension, and with better retention.

- Daily, *read* the textbook. Too many students will purchase an expensive textbook yet never even open it! Or, if they do, they just skim the material and don't read it. It is usually recommended to read the material before you get to class (even if it doesn't make sense to you). But even if you don't, simply read the material after class. Reading a textbook can often times be boring, cumbersome, and confusing. Therefore, read in short increments (15 minutes here and there). If something confuses you, read it again and think about the concept. If it is still confusing, be sure to ask the instructor about it either during class, in office hours, or via email. As you read your book, only spend your time reading the *assigned* text and focus on the material that is talked about in class (otherwise, you will get overwhelmed with material). Take notes while you read the book. And finally, look at the pictures and read the captions. The images (and figures and tables) are there for a reason. Most students are visual learners. Use the visual aids that accompany the written material.

- Study questions (problem sets or homework): Any study guide, problem set, or homework assignment should be immediately addressed. Often times it is best to read these questions prior to reading the text. This way, you will have key words, points, and concepts to look for in the text. In addition, read these questions before coming to class; you will then know exactly what to listen for in class. You should approach problems via the following method: First, you need to understand exactly what the question is asking. If you understand the question you will be better able to answer it. Second, when you answer the question you need to understand the answer. Often times, students "find" an answer in the textbook or in the notes and assume the task is complete. But if you copy down an answer for the sake of completing an assignment, you will most likely *not* be successful on the exams. You need to read the question and understand it. You then need to have a thoughtful answer that you understand. Critical thinking questions such as the ones found in this book require a lot of thinking and comprehension. If you don't initially understand something, then you must think and then think again. In addition, try to answer the questions in your own words (rather than verbatim with the textbook or the notes). To truly test you understanding, try to answer the question without referring to the answer that you have written down. Can you explain the question/answer without looking at your notes? If you can, then you will be successful.

- Memorization. Some material does require memorization. Memorization takes time and commitment. Memorize material in small increments. Constantly test yourself such that you won't forget. Also, to memorize means *not* to rely on your notes. Force yourself to remember information *without* looking at your notes.

- Preparation for exam: You should be in constant, daily preparation. *Do not* wait until the last minute to study. Follow the guidelines above.

- Finally, foster an appreciation for the material that you are studying. Note its importance to you and to the world. Also note what studying this material it's doing for you: By understanding this material you are learning how to think critically. You are learning how to *think*. With your success here, you are conditioning yourself to be a life-long learner; to make good, thoughtful decisions, and to be a leader. Believe it or not.

Part 1: Basics of Physical Geography

Chapter 1: Latitude, Longitude, Time
Chapter 2: Solar Angle and the Seasons

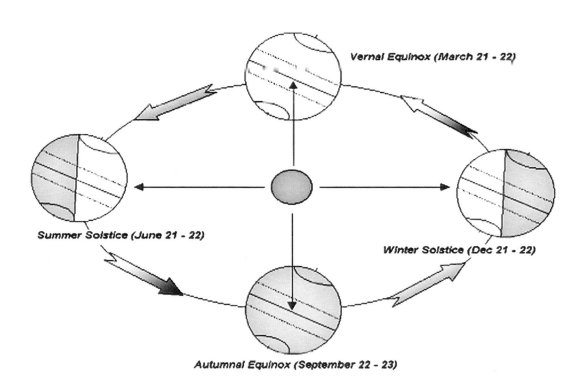

Vernal Equinox (March 21 - 22)

Summer Solstice (June 21 - 22)

Winter Solstice (Dec 21 - 22)

Autumnal Equinox (September 22 - 23)

Chapter 1: Latitude, Longitude, Time

1. How can you prove that the Earth is round, without using modern technology?

This seems like a difficult question. As with many problems, however, once you know some basic concepts it is not as difficult as it first appears. The "Pythagoreans" in 600 B.C. realized that the Earth was spherical by observing lunar eclipses. A lunar eclipse is when the Moon is "eclipsed" by Earth's shadow:

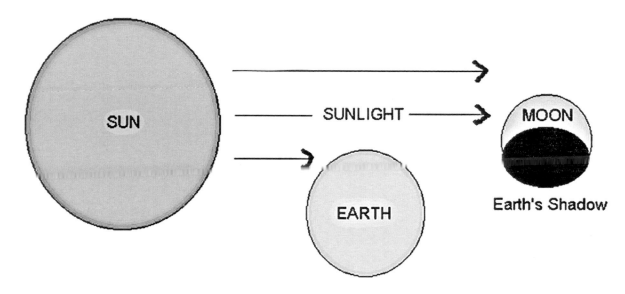

The Pythagoreans realized that there is only one geometric shape in which no matter the angle of light striking that shape, the shadow cast will always be circular; that shape is a sphere. Therefore, because lunar eclipses *always* show a circular (or, curved) shadow of the Earth on the Moon, the Earth *must* be a sphere.

2. If it is 11am, Saturday, at a location of 135°E longitude, what time and day is it at 165°W?

The Earth rotates counterclockwise a total of 360° every 24 hours ("counterclockwise" means that if you looking down upon Earth from above the North Pole, the Earth will be rotating in a direction opposite to the hands on a clock). So, the Earth rotates 360° per 24 hours = 360/24 = 15° of rotation per hour. In other words, after 1 hour of time the Earth has rotated an additional 15° of longitude. Each time zone, therefore, is 1 hour long *or* 15° of longitude wide.

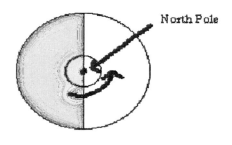

Because the Earth is rotating counterclockwise (in an easterly direction), any location *east of you* is *ahead* in time. Any location *west of you* is *behind* in time (see Figure 1 below). In other words, Earth rotates from west to east ("easterly" direction); therefore, the Sun rises in the east and sets in the west. If the Sun rises in the east, that means that for anyone east of *you* the Sun is rising for them *before* it rises for you. Thus, they are ahead of you in time. Take a globe and shine a flashlight above San Diego – pretend this is the Sun. The point directly below the light is solar noon; the point east of the light (i.e., over the central U.S.) is afternoon; and the point west of the light (over the Pacific Ocean) is before noon. Rotate the globe and notice how the Pacific Ocean rotates *into* noon as San Diego rotates out of noon.

FIGURE 1
Diagram Showing Time Differences
The Sun *rises* in the *east* and *sets* in the *west*. In the example below, the time for the person at the Prime Meridian is solar noon. For the person standing in the east, the time is *after*noon. For the person standing in the west, the time is *before* noon (notice for the person standing in the west, that the Sun is in the *eastern*, rising sky and for the person standing in the east, the Sun is in the *western*, setting sky).

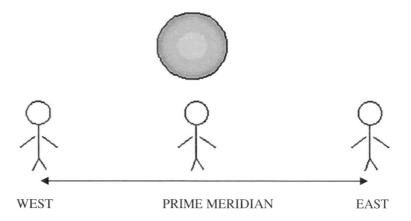

WEST   PRIME MERIDIAN   EAST

So, we know that every 15° of longitude equals 1 hour of time. We also know that a location *west* of you is *behind* in time, and a location *east* of you is *ahead* in time. Now, all we need to do is determine the number of degrees of longitude that separate 135° East from 165° West, and then divide this number by 15:

Note: 165 West + 135 East = 300 degrees. And, 300/15 = 20 hours. So, 165° West is 20 hours *behind* 135° East. Therefore, the time and day at 165° West is: 11 am, Saturday *minus* 20 hours = 3 pm, Friday (use your fingers to count if you have to!).

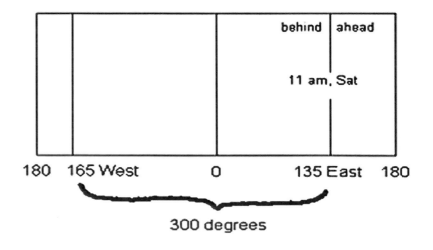

To answer the above question, we counted 20 hours behind 135° East. In fact, we could have answered the question just as well by counting *ahead* rather than behind (remember, we live on a sphere, not a disc!). If 165° West is 20 hours *behind* 135° East, then it is also *4 hours ahead* of 135° East. Remember, we live on a sphere with a total of 24 time zones. Therefore, *time ahead + time behind = 24*. So, if the time and day at 135° East is 11 am, Saturday, then: 11 am, Saturday + 4 hours = 3 pm. But, how do we determine the day? If you start at 135°E and travel east toward 165°W then you will cross over the International Date Line (180°). If you cross over the Date Line from the eastern hemisphere *to the* western hemisphere, then you gain a day (set the calendar back). If you cross over the Date Line from the western hemisphere *to the* eastern hemisphere, then you lose a day (set the calendar ahead).

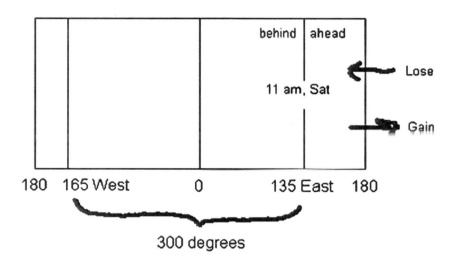

3. It is solar noon at your *unknown* longitude. Your chronometer (clock) reads 8 a.m. (your clock is set to Pacific Standard Time at 120° West Longitude). So, what is your longitude?

In essence, this problem is a time-zone problem similar to Question #2 above. The same rules apply; Earth makes one complete rotation of 360° in 24 hours, therefore, the world rotates at a rate of 15° per hour. Subsequently, every 1 hour of time translates into 15° of longitude. First, we need to determine two things: 1) is noon ahead or behind of 8 a.m.; and 2) how many hours

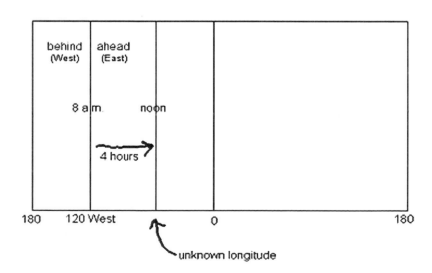

separate 8 a.m. from noon? We can set up the problem as follows (see diagram to the right): We determine that noon is *ahead* of 8 a.m. by 4 hours; that is, anyone living to the east of 120° West has already experienced noon. For them, it is now *afternoon*. Why? Remember, the Earth rotates in a counterclockwise direction – or, toward the east. This is why the Sun rises in the east and sets in the west. Any location to the east of any other location will *always* be ahead in time. Therefore, we know that our unknown location is 4 hours east of 120° West longitude. Every 1 hour equates to 15° of longitude, therefore: 4 hours x 15° = 60°. We determine that the unknown location is 60° east of 120° West. Therefore, the unknown location is 120° - 60° = 60° West Longitude.

Bonus Question: Imagine that you set your watch at local noon in Kansas City on Monday and then fly to the *Coast* on Tuesday. You stick a pole into the ground on a sunny day at the beach, wait until its shadow is shortest, and look at your watch. The watch says 10:00 am. Are you on the East Coast or West Coast of the United States?

Answer: East Coast.

4. You go outside and determine that the North Celestial Pole star (Polaris) is 30 degrees above your northern horizon. So, what is your latitude?

Living on a sphere poses certain problems with regards to navigation. For example, what if you wanted to travel from San Diego, CA to London, England? What path would you take? Which direction yields the shortest distance? The shortest distance between any two points is a straight line. But how do you draw a straight line on a globe? For that matter, how can you navigate upon a sphere, at all? Certainly, traveling to London, England is not as simple as saying, "Take a right turn at the Atlantic Ocean."

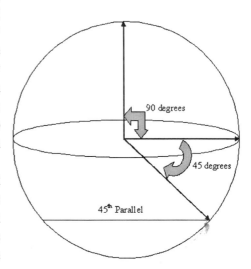

The way that we have overcome this apparent problem is with the *geographic grid*. The geographic grid divides the world into both northern/southern components (*latitude*) and eastern/western components (*longitude*). The range of latitude is from 0° (the Equator) to 90° North and South Latitude. The range of longitude is from 0° (the Prime Meridian) to 180° (the International Date Line, which can be gotten to by either going east or west). Lines of latitude are known as *parallels*. Lines of longitude are known as *meridians*.

Every place on Earth has a geographic grid coordinate. For example, San Diego, California is located at 32° North Latitude, 117° West Longitude. Note: the image on the right is Earth from above the North Pole.

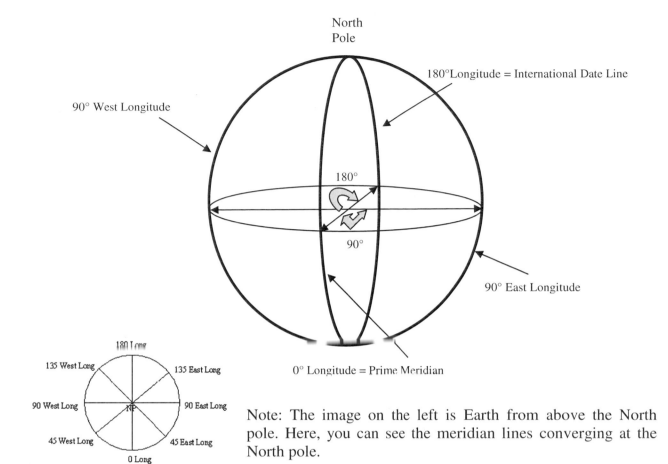

Note: The image on the left is Earth from above the North pole. Here, you can see the meridian lines converging at the North pole.

The use of the North Celestial Pole star for navigation purposes has been used for thousands of years. In particular, the position of the North Star (Polaris) will tell you your latitude (whereas a good clock will help you to determine your longitude -- see Question #3 above).

In order to answer this question, you must remember one very important concept; the Earth rotates on its axis in a counterclockwise or, easterly direction. Because Earth is rotating in an easterly direction, all of the stars in the nighttime sky appear to move during the evening from the east toward the west (just like the Sun does

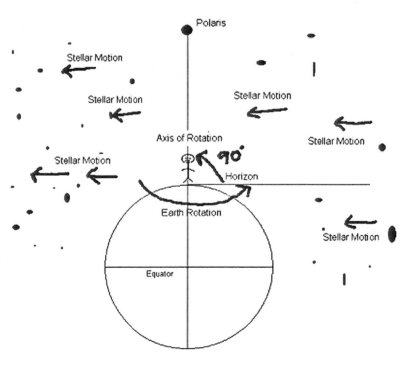

during the course of the day). This is true for all of the stars *except* for Polaris. Polaris resides on Earth's axis of rotation, and as such, does not appear to move in the evening sky, at all.

=As the diagram above depicts, all of the stars in the sky (except for Polaris) appear to rise in the east and set in the west due to fact that Earth is rotating counterclockwise (we use the term "appear" because in reality it is not the stars revolving around the Earth, but rather the Earth rotating on its axis giving the stars their "apparent" motion). Polaris does not appear to move because it is directly on Earth's axis of rotation.

Now, in order to find your latitude, all you need to do is determine the angle that Polaris makes with your north horizon. For someone standing on the North Pole, the angle that Polaris makes with his/her horizon is 90°; therefore, the North Pole is located at 90° North Latitude.

For someone in San Diego, California, the angle that Polaris makes with his/her north horizon is 32°. Therefore, residents of San Diego, CA are located at 32° North Latitude. So, if someone sees that Polaris is 30° above their north horizon, then that person is located at 30° North Latitude.

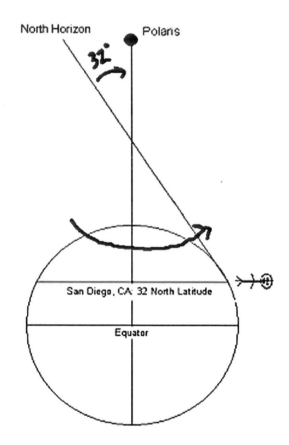

Bonus Question: Can someone in the Southern Hemisphere use Polaris to locate his/her latitude? Why or why not?

Answer: No. If you are in the Southern Hemisphere, then the North Star (Polaris) will be *below* your horizon. You will not see it and therefore not be able to use it to track your position. Rather, you must use the South Celestial Pole Star.

Chapter 2: Solar Angle and the Seasons

1. If the Earth had no tilt how many seasons would exist on Earth? What if the Earth had a 90° tilt, how many seasons?

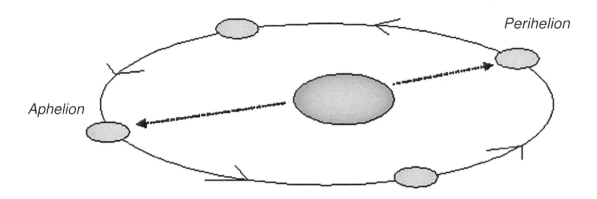

　　　　The above diagram depicts Earth as it orbits the Sun. The orbit is not completely circular but elliptical. An elliptical orbit means that there will be a period of time when Earth is *closest to the Sun* (perihelion) and a period of time when Earth is *farthest from the Sun* (aphelion). During perihelion the Earth is 91 million miles away from the Sun. During aphelion the Earth is 93 million miles away from the Sun. Interestingly, the date of perihelion is January 3 and the date of aphelion is July 3. In other words, during the Northern Hemisphere winter, the Earth is actually *closest* to the Sun! And, during the Northern Hemisphere summer, the Earth is actually *farthest* from the Sun. Therefore, it is not Earth's proximity to the Sun that gives us our seasons; rather it is Earth's 23.5° tilt (see image below).

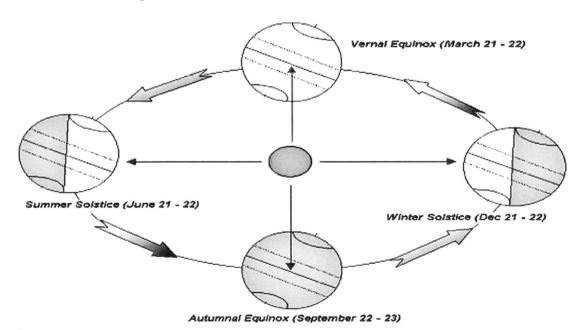

Notice in the diagram that during the summer, the tilt of the Earth is toward the Sun. During the winter, the tilt of the Earth is away from the Sun. During the Fall or Spring (Autumnal Equinox for Fall; Vernal Equinox for Spring), the tilt of the Earth is parallel to the Sun.

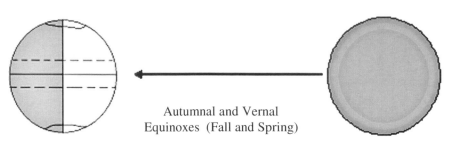

Autumnal and Vernal Equinoxes (Fall and Spring)

In the diagrams, the shaded portion of the Earth represents nighttime. For the image of the summer solstice, the Earth's tilt is such that anywhere above the Arctic Circle (66.5°N. Lat.), there are 24 hours of daylight. Yet during the winter solstice, the Earth's tilt is such that anywhere above the Arctic Circle, there are 24 hours of night. During both equinoxes, there are 12 hours of daylight and 12 hours of night everywhere in the world. One of the major components to seasonal variation is the length of daylight hours. We can see from the diagrams that summer is marked by *increased* daylight hours; winter is marked by *decreased* daylight hours; and Fall/Spring is marked by equal amounts of daylight and nighttime hours. The fluctuation of daytime hours is a direct result of the tilt of the Earth coupled with Earth's revolution around the Sun. So, what if the Earth was tilted 0° (no tilt)?

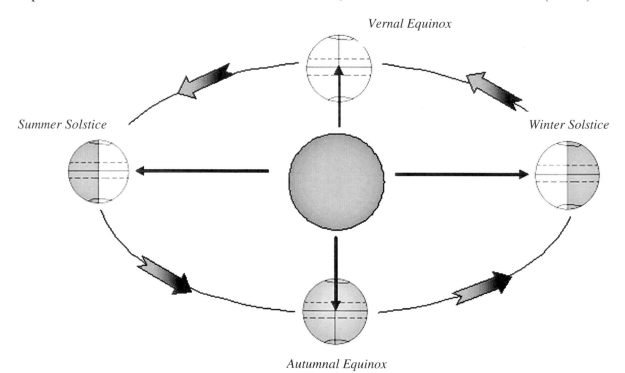

Vernal Equinox

Summer Solstice

Winter Solstice

Autumnal Equinox

As the above image depicts, if we were to remove the tilt of the Earth, we would be removing the seasons. For every single day of the year – at every location on Earth – there would be 12 hours of daylight and 12 hours of nighttime. In other words, no tilt would lead to *no* seasonal change. The only slight seasonal variation that would occur would be due to the small distance changes of the Earth relative to the Sun (perihelion and aphelion).

Answer: There would be *one* perpetual season (very similar to Fall and Spring).

What if the Earth had a 90° tilt rather than a 23.5° tilt?

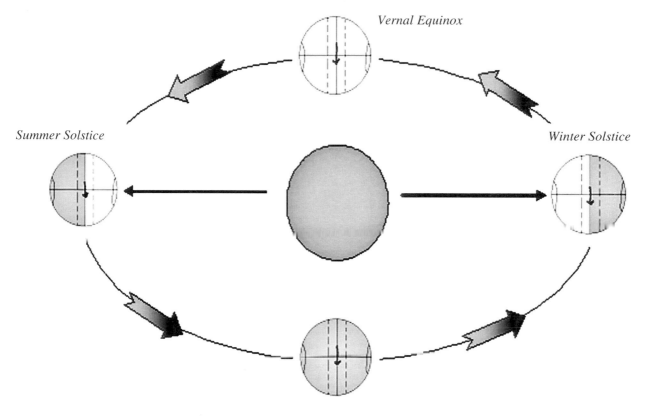

Take a *close* look at the diagram above. The arrows drawn on the Earth indicate the direction of Earth's rotation (always counterclockwise when viewed from above the North Pole). As you would expect, during the summer solstice, the Northern Hemisphere is tilted toward the Sun. But the tilt is not 23.5°; rather, it is a full 90°! Not only is it summer time in the Northern Hemisphere (and winter in the Southern Hemisphere), but it is an *extreme* summer. As depicted in the diagram, every location above the equator (from 0° to 90° North Latitude) would have 24 hours of daylight! During the winter solstice every location above the equator (from 0° to 90° North Latitude) would have 24 hours of nighttime! During the Autumnal and Vernal equinox the picture will look like the diagram below (notice Earth's counterclockwise rotation as viewed from above the North Pole). Also notice the 12 hours of daylight and 12 hours of nighttime everywhere on Earth (just like what we have with the 23.5° tilt):

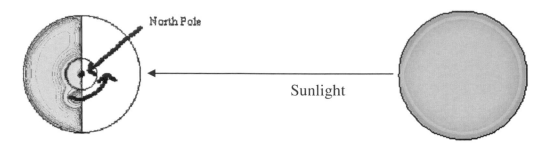

Answer: A 90° tilt will still produce four seasons on Earth (as a matter of fact, *any* tilt -- no matter how big or small -- will still create four seasons). With a 90° tilt, the summer and winter, however, would be *very* extreme. Fall and spring on the other hand would be similar to what they are today (with reference to length of daylight and position of the Sun in the sky).

2. How many times is the Sun *directly* overhead Ecuador during the *year*?

In the diagram below, notice how the position of the Sun migrates during the course of the year from 23.5° North (the summer solstice) to 23.5° South (the winter solstice). During the summer solstice, the solar rays (at solar noon) are striking directly on top of the Tropic of Cancer (located at 23.5° North latitude). During the winter solstice, the solar rays (at solar noon) are striking directly on top of the Tropic of Capricorn (23.5° South latitude). During the autumnal and vernal equinoxes, the solar rays (at solar noon) are striking directly on top of the Equator (0° latitude).

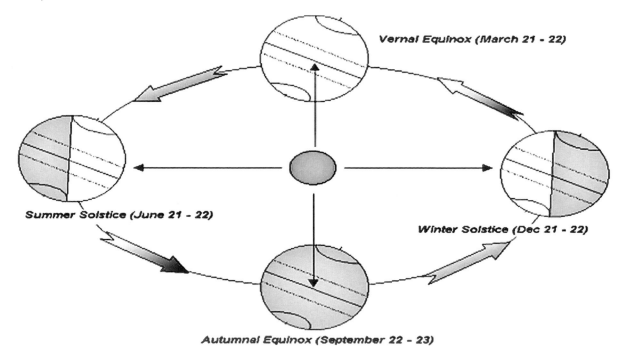

During the course of the year, therefore, the Sun will "cross" over the Equator two times (once during the autumnal equinox and once during the vernal equinox). Thus, the Sun will be *directly* overhead Ecuador *twice* a year (Ecuador is located at 0° latitude).

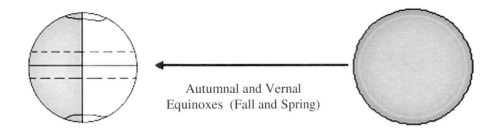

Autumnal and Vernal
Equinoxes (Fall and Spring)

What exactly does this mean? Essentially, if you were in Quito, Ecuador, during either of the seasonal equinoxes, at solar noon the Sun would be directly overhead with no shadows cast. The days of the vernal and autumnal equinox are the only two days during the year when this will happen. On all other days at the Equator, if you were to go outside at solar noon, the Sun would *not* be directly overhead. Rather, it would be as much as 23.5° North or South from being overhead (dependent upon the day of the year).

3. On the date of the Winter Solstice (December 21) you find yourself on a beach in San Diego, California (32° North Latitude). The time is approximately solar noon. You look toward the southern sky and see the Sun. How many degrees above the southern horizon (solar angle) is the Sun? What is the solar zenith angle?

The key to solving this problem and others like it is *visualization*. If you can draw the picture, you can solve the problem. Of course, before you draw the picture, you need to know a few concepts first. To begin with, let us define *solar zenith angle* and *solar angle*. Solar zenith angle is the angle that the Sun makes with your zenith point. Solar angle is the angle that the Sun makes with your horizon (see diagram below):

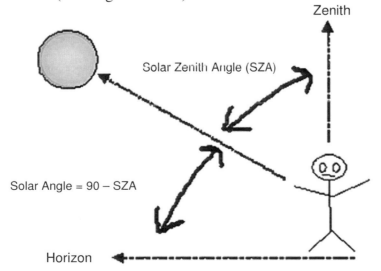

Before we can draw the picture and solve the given problem, there is one more question that we must first address: *What is the importance of knowing the date and time?* By knowing the date and time, we will be able to place the Sun in the sky and determine both the solar zenith angle and the solar angle. The question notes that the date is the winter solstice. On the day of the winter solstice (December 21), the Sun is located at its southern most point, having a Declination of -23°, or, 23° South (shining directly above the Tropic of Capricorn). What exactly does this mean? As Earth revolves around the Sun, the *apparent position* of the Sun in the sky shifts toward the north or toward the south dependent upon the season. In the diagrams below, notice where the most vertical rays of the Sun are striking the Earth during each season. During the summer solstice (June 21), the Sun is at its northern most point during the year, having a Declination of +23°, or, 23° North (shining directly above the Tropic of Cancer). In other words, if you lived somewhere on the Tropic of Cancer and you went outside at solar noon during the day of the summer solstice, the Sun would be *directly* over your head. For you (at the Tropic of Cancer) this is the *only* day during the course of the year when this will happen. For all other days, the Sun will *not* be at your zenith point at solar noon. Solar noon is when the Sun is at its *highest* point in the sky for *your location* during that day (rarely does this mean that the Sun is directly overhead). During either the vernal equinox (March 21) or the autumnal equinox (September 21), the Sun is located at a Declination of 0° (shining directly above the Equator). Please refer to the diagrams below. The first image shows Earth in its yearly orbit around the Sun. The second set of images provides a close-up view of the Earth during the solstices and equinoxes.

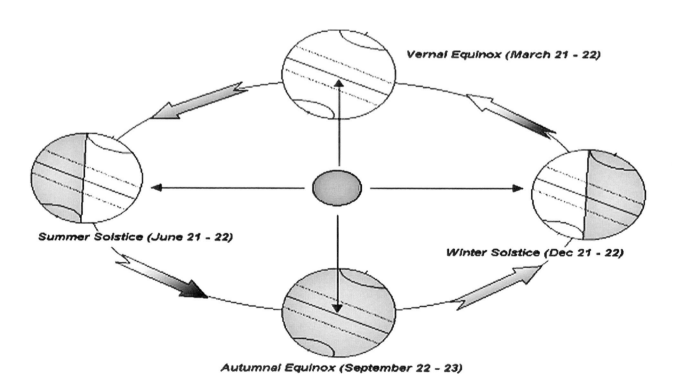

Vernal Equinox (March 21 - 22)

Summer Solstice (June 21 - 22)

Winter Solstice (Dec 21 - 22)

Autumnal Equinox (September 22 - 23)

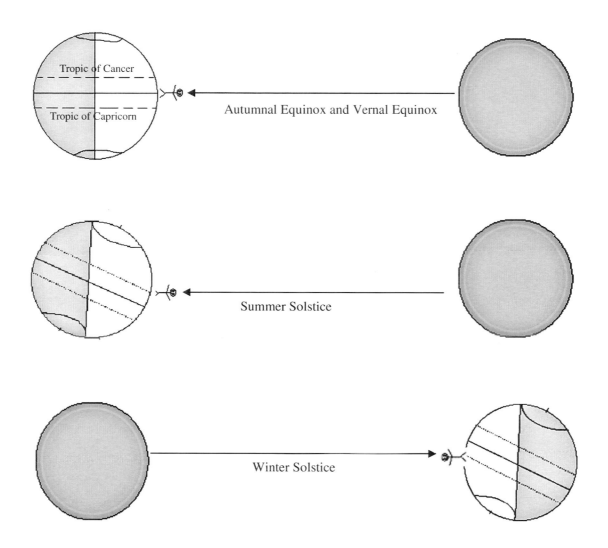

The diagrams above provide you with everything you need to solve the problem. Let us first write down exactly what the question *gives* us: 1) Date = Winter Solstice. Or, the Sun is located at 23° South (shining directly on top of the Tropic of Capricorn at solar noon); 2) Location = San Diego, California (Latitude = 32° North); 3) Time = solar noon. Now, let's draw the picture:

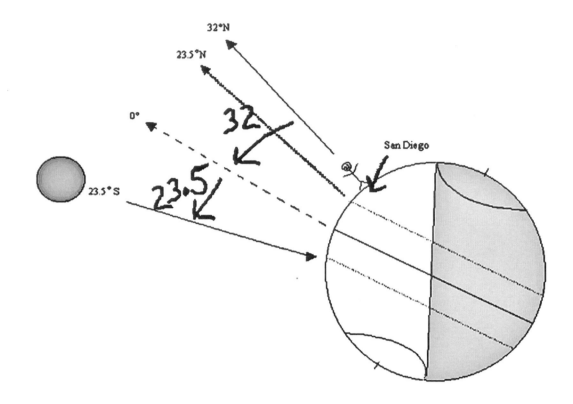

According to the diagram above the date is the winter solstice (notice that the Sun is shining directly above the Tropic of Capricorn at 23.5° South Latitude), and you are standing somewhere in San Diego, CA (notice that your zenith point is 32° North Latitude). The picture also shows the zenith point for the Equator (0° Latitude) and the Tropic of Cancer (23.5° North Latitude for reference). So, all we need to do is read the diagram: the solar zenith angle is 32° + 23.5° = 55.5° (that is, the angle that your zenith point makes with the Sun is 55.5°). Therefore, the solar angle is 90° - 55.5° = 34.5°. Note: during the course of the day (on this day), the Sun will be no higher than 34.5° above your southern horizon; or, 55.5° from zenith.

The shift of the Declination of the Sun during the course of the year explains, in part, the reason why we have seasons; the more vertical the solar rays, the warmer the conditions. Why? It's a flashlight phenomenon. If you point a flashlight straight down, most of the light is concentrated over a small surface area. If you point a flashlight at an angle, the light is now distributed over a greater surface area. So, during the summer, the flashlight is shining as close to straight down as it will be during the course of the year (at your location). During the winter, the flashlight is shining down at a much more oblique angle. The following diagram depicts the position of the Sun (solar Declination) at solar noon on the summer solstice (June 21), the winter solstice (December 21), and the vernal and autumnal equinoxes (March 21 and September 21, respectively). Note the position of the Sun (throughout the year) relative to someone living in San Diego, CA:

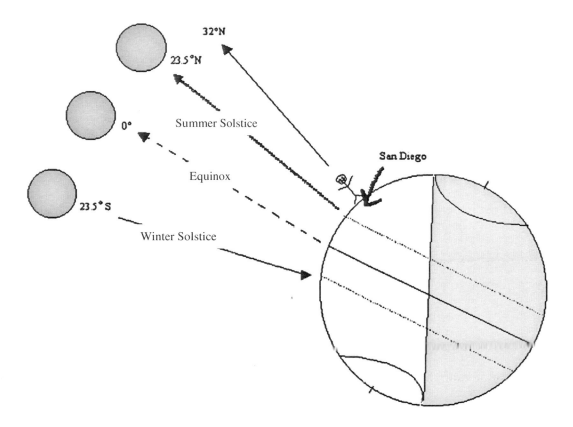

Bonus Question: If the date is the summer solstice (June 21) what is the solar zenith angle?

Answer: Using the above diagram we note that the difference in the zenith point of the Sun (solar Declination) during the summer solstice versus the zenith point for someone living in San Diego is 8.5° (32° - 23.5°). What is the solar zenith angle during an equinox or the winter solstice?

4. As you go to higher latitude how does the length of daylight hours change?

Let us once again refer back to the diagrams from the previous questions. According to the diagrams, if the date is the summer solstice, the length of daylight hours *increase* as you go to higher latitudes. In fact, if you are at a location north of the Arctic Circle (66.5°N. Latitude), during the summer solstice you will receive 24 hours of daylight! However, if the date is the winter solstice, as you go to higher latitudes the length of daylight hours *decreases*. Take a close look at the winter solstice picture. If you are at a location north of the Arctic Circle, you will receive 24 hours of night on this day! Finally, during either the autumnal or vernal equinox, *all* latitudes will receive 12 hours of daylight and 12 hours of night.

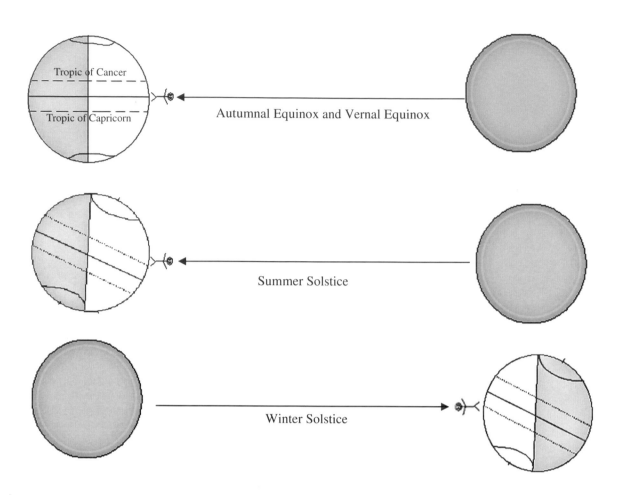

5. Directly after the date of the autumnal equinox, and as the Earth continues to revolve around the Sun, how are daylight hours in the *Southern Hemisphere* changing?

Refer back to the diagrams in Question #2 through 4 above. Find the position of the *circle of illumination* (the line that separates night from day). During the summer solstice, everywhere *above* the Equator has *more than* 12 hours of daylight; everywhere *below* the Equator has *more than* 12 hours of night. The situation is reversed during the winter solstice. During the equinoxes there are 12 hours of daylight and 12 hours of night *everywhere* on Earth.

According to the diagrams, therefore, after the autumnal equinox, and as the Earth continues to revolve around the Sun (notice the counterclockwise revolution of Earth around the Sun), daytime hours are *decreasing* in the Northern Hemisphere as the winter solstice approaches. In the Southern Hemisphere, however, daylight hours are *increasing* (residents of the Southern Hemisphere are approaching their summer solstice whereas residents of the Northern Hemisphere are approaching their winter solstice).

6. You want to determine your latitude. The date is the vernal equinox (March 21). On this day, the solar declination is 0°. When you go outside (on this day at solar noon), you notice that the Sun is 75° above your *southern* horizon. With this information, determine your latitude.

The developing theme of this section is to *draw the picture*. Even if you have no idea what to do (!), if you can draw the picture, perhaps the answer will simply "fall out" (see diagram below):

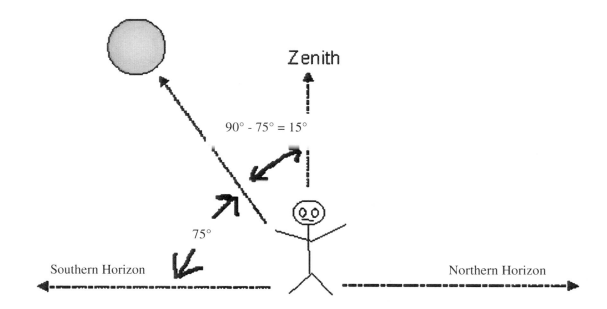

According to our diagram above, if the Sun is 75° *above* the southern horizon (this is the *solar angle*), then the solar zenith angle *must be* 15° (remember, the total angle from zenith to the horizon = the solar angle + the solar zenith angle = 90°; for an example of calculating the solar zenith angle, please refer back to Question #3). According to the question, therefore, on the date of the vernal equinox, the Sun is 15° *south* of zenith (see diagram below):

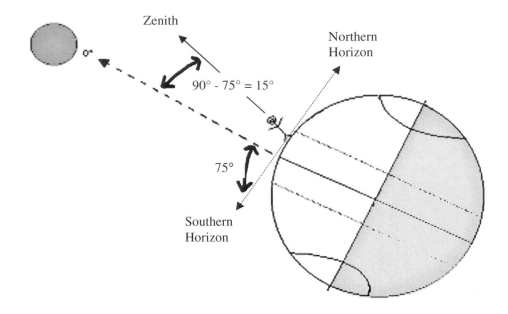

Answer: The unknown Latitude is 15° North Latitude.

7. Why does moss generally grow on the north side of trees?

Here, we must be careful when using the word "generally". The fact of the matter is moss will grow on whatever side of the tree it needs to, dependent upon nutrient and moisture availability. Moss requires a lot of moisture. If the Sun is always in the southern sky, for example, then south-facing slopes (i.e., on mountains) will experience enough solar radiation to evaporate moisture at a relatively high rate. Thus, vegetation will be sparse. The adjacent north-facing slopes will have more moisture available due to less evaporation from solar radiation. Thus, vegetation can be more abundant. The same idea holds true for trees. If a tree is at a location in which more moisture is available on its north face versus its south face, then moss will grow on the north face. *Any* latitude in the Northern Hemisphere north of the Tropic of Cancer (23.5° North Latitude) will *always* have the Sun in the southern sky. Therefore, if moss is going to grow, it will typically grow on the north side, where solar radiation (and subsequent evaporation) is less than the south side. Of course, in very rainy environments, both sides of the tree will receive an abundance of moisture; therefore, the position of the Sun in the sky is less important. The diagram below depicts the location of the Sun (solar Declination) during the solstices and the equinoxes. Notice that the Sun *never* has a solar Declination greater than 23.5° North or South.

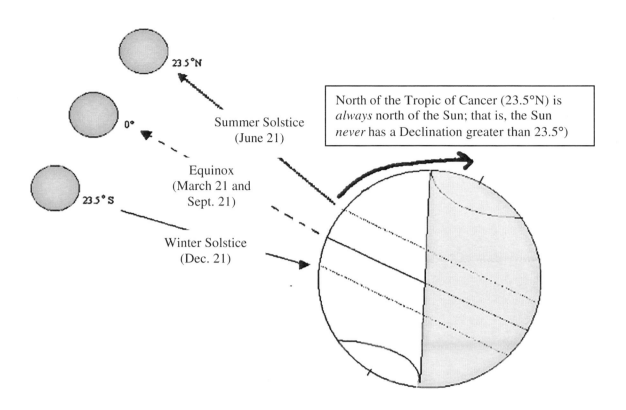

North of the Tropic of Cancer (23.5°N) is *always* north of the Sun; that is, the Sun *never* has a Declination greater than 23.5°)

23.5°N

0°

23.5°S

Summer Solstice
(June 21)

Equinox
(March 21 and
Sept. 21)

Winter Solstice
(Dec. 21)

Part 2: The Atmosphere

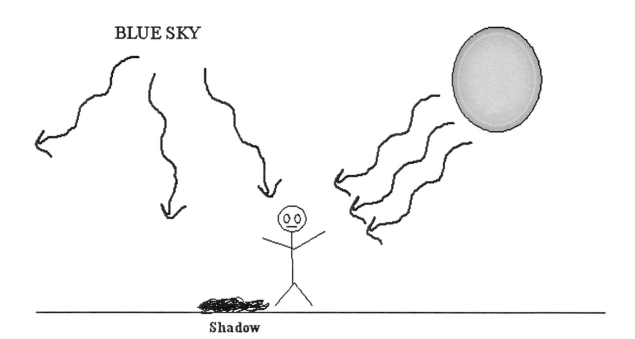

BLUE SKY

Shadow

Chapter 3: Electromagnetic Radiation, Energy, and the Atmosphere

1. If ozone blocks Ultraviolet (UV) light, and if UV light is responsible for suntans and sunburns, how can you get a suntan or a sunburn?

It is true that ozone (O_3) absorbs (or, blocks) UV light. However, there is not enough ozone in the stratosphere to block 100% of the incoming UV rays. Therefore, the relatively small amount of UV light that penetrates through the atmosphere provides us with our suntans and our sunburns. So, what exactly is a suntan or a sunburn? Remember, UV rays are high energy photons emanating from the Sun. They are so high energy, in fact, that large enough quantities of UV, upon striking your skin, can actually cause cellular mutations (i.e., the structure of skin molecules gets broken down by the UV). The cellular mutation causes the skin to change colors. In the case of a suntan, the skin turns brown. In the case of a sunburn, the skin turns red. In other words, both a suntan and a sunburn cause cellular mutation. The sunburn is just more extreme (and damaging) to the skin than the suntan. Either way, it is best *not* to expose yourself to too much UV. If you are outside a lot, wearing UV protection such as high SPF lotion is a good idea. Also remember, that UV light *easily* penetrates through cloud cover. So, even during a cloudy day, one can still obtain a suntan or a sunburn. The image below shows the path of UV through the atmosphere. A large amount of UV waves are absorbed by ozone within the Stratosphere. What doesn't get absorbed makes its way through the Troposphere to the surface of the Earth.

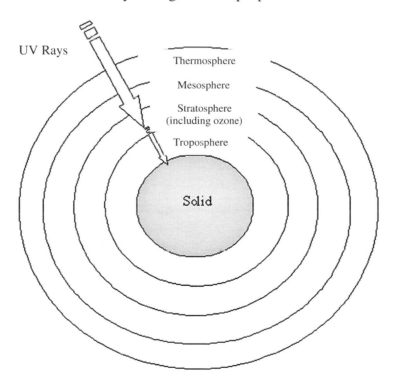

2. In the thermosphere, individual gas molecules absorb high-energy radiation (namely, x-rays) and therefore have high temperatures, but *heat* (the *total* energy in the thermosphere) is low. Why? If you were flying through the thermosphere (only in regular clothes, like superman), would you freeze or fry?

Atmospheric gases (like everything else on Earth) are attracted to Earth via gravity. Of course, other forces at work prevent a massive atmospheric collapse inward! Nevertheless, because of gravity, the majority of atmospheric gases are actually found in the troposphere. As you go higher into the sky, the quantity of atmospheric gases becomes less and less:

480.000 m

80.000 m	**THERMOSPHERE**
50.000 m	**MESOSPHERE**
17,000 m	**STRATOSPHERE**
0 meters (m)	**TROPOSPHERE**

Gases in the thermosphere absorb high-energy radiation that emanates from the Sun (predominately, x-rays). Therefore, individual gas molecules in the thermosphere are extremely hot (over 1600°F!). However, *heat* is relatively low. Heat is defined as the *total* amount of energy within a system. Because there are so few gas molecules present in the thermosphere, even though the individual gas molecules are hot, the *overall* heat in the thermosphere is low. Thus, if you were to fly around the thermosphere (like superman), you would actually freeze. The only way you could fry is if you were to continually bang into the very hot gas molecules. But because the gas molecules are so few and far between, your chances of frying are rather slim.

3. Imagine you are standing in the Antarctic during the Southern Hemisphere summer. The sky is clear and blue. There are no clouds in the sky. Your shadow is cast on the icy ground. What is the color of your shadow?

First of all, what causes a shadow? A shadow is the result of an object blocking the path of light. Because the object blocks the path of the light source, the resultant shadow is generally black (or gray). Therefore, how can a shadow be any color other than black or gray? *Answer*: In order for a shadow to be a color other than black or gray, there *must* be another source of light that can essentially cast its glow on the resultant shadow. This is exactly what happens (quite often) in the Antarctic.

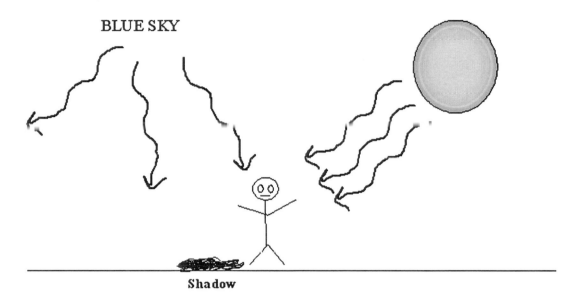

In the picture above notice that there are two sources of light: 1) the Sun; and 2) the sky. According to the question, both sources of light are quite bright. Remember, the sky is blue due to Rayleigh Scattering. Rayleigh Scattering occurs when blue light is scattered by relatively small sized gases in the atmosphere (namely, oxygen and nitrogen). In addition to Rayleigh Scattering, there is also Mie Scattering. Mie Scattering occurs when red light is scattered by relatively large sized atmospheric gases (such as carbon dioxide, photochemical smog, and aerosols). The more Mie Scattering that occurs, the less blue the sky will appear (as the blue light is subdued by the reds). Because the sky in the Antarctic is generally devoid of photochemical smog and atmospheric aerosols, the sky is typically deep blue; so deep as a matter of fact that when the light of the Sun is blocked out, a beautiful blue glow can actually be seen on the ground. Of course, in the modern city, this blue glow won't be seen due to the fact that the Rayleigh Scattering is tempered by Mie Scattering (i.e., lots of "stuff" in the sky).

Bonus Question: At high altitudes is the sky above a deeper blue or a pale blue versus lower altitudes?

Answer: At high altitudes the sky is a deeper blue versus lower altitudes. Review the answer above (and the answer to the next question) if you are uncertain as to why.

4. Why can we look directly at the Sun at sunrise and sunset but not at noon (or other times during the middle of the day)?

The figure below depicts the Sun at sunrise, solar noon, and sunset. Notice that during sunrise and sunset, solar radiation passes through a greater amount of troposphere than at solar noon. As one goes from sea level to the upper atmosphere, the quantity of gases in the sky *decreases* exponentially (see Question #2 above). This means, that the majority of atmospheric gases in the atmosphere are found in the troposphere. Because the path of solar radiation goes through so much troposphere during sunrise and sunset, a good proportion of this radiation will get absorbed, scattered, and refracted by the atmosphere (this is the principle reason for red and orange sunsets/sunrises; most of the blue has been scattered out). This is why the Sun appears both bigger and dimmer during sunrise and sunset (by the way, you still don't want to look at the Sun directly and/or for long periods of time, as you can still burn your optics!). At solar noon, the Sun is at its highest point in the sky. Radiation passes through less atmosphere. Therefore, the Sun will appear smaller but much brighter.

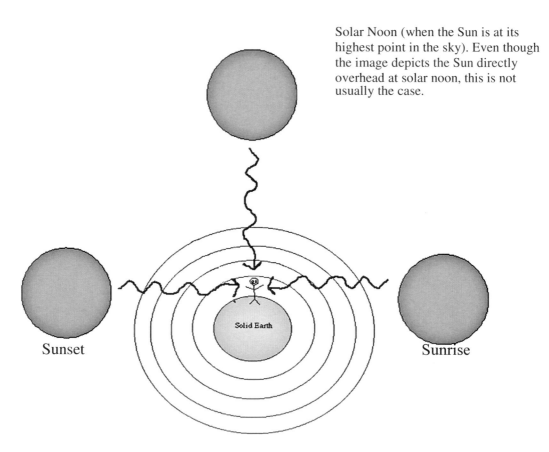

Solar Noon (when the Sun is at its highest point in the sky). Even though the image depicts the Sun directly overhead at solar noon, this is not usually the case.

Sunset

Sunrise

Solid Earth

5. With your understanding of why the sky is blue (and why the sky has other atmospheric colors), answer the following question: Why do you think the lunar (Moon) sky is black?

In order for there to be atmospheric colors there must be an atmosphere! Rayleigh Scattering occurs when blue light is scattered by atmospheric gases such as oxygen and nitrogen, and Mie Scattering occurs when red light is scattered by atmospheric gases such as carbon dioxide. By the way, with added "ingredients" in the sky such as smog, scattering can produce beautiful pinks and oranges. The key to any color is atmosphere. If an atmosphere does not exist, no colors will be scattered or reflected by the atmosphere. If this is the case, the atmosphere will remain black, as is the case with the Moon.

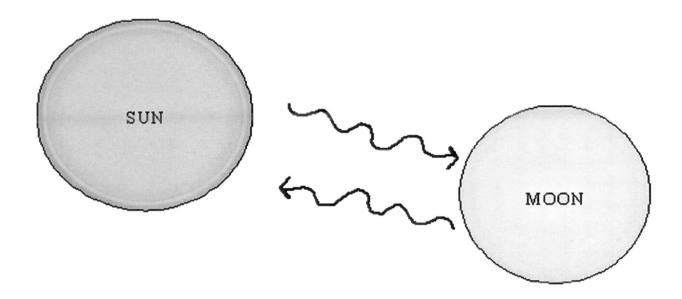

The majority of solar radiation flows – unimpeded -- through the lunar sky because there is no atmosphere. The radiation then reflects off the surface of the Moon, bouncing back into space. Because the Moon has no atmosphere to reflect, refract, or scatter radiation, the sky remains black (i.e., no Rayleigh, Mie, or non-selective scattering).

Chapter 4: Atmospheric Temperature

1. If our Earth did not have an atmosphere, how would temperature extremes vary between day and night?

The atmosphere is truly the key to our existence. Without it, we would have no air to breath, water to drink, or food to earth. Without an atmosphere our planet would not have the ability to retain solar energy within the system. Heat on our planet is a direct result of solar radiation. However, without an atmosphere there would be no way for the planet to keep the solar energy within the system for any lengthy period of time. Compare the two diagrams below. With an atmosphere, the differences in temperature between day and night are *relatively* minimal. During the day, solar radiation is absorbed within the Earth system. As the ground heats up, the radiation is then sent upward, into the atmosphere. Atmospheric gases absorb this heat energy and radiate it back down toward the solid Earth. At night, the ground cools off (no more solar radiation to heat up the ground), yet heat that had been absorbed during the day continues to radiate from the ground to the atmosphere (albeit, becoming less and less throughout the evening). The atmosphere, therefore, keeps the energy in the system for a relatively long period of time. The differences in day versus night temperatures are kept at a minimum. Of course, if we had no atmosphere, there would be no way for the solar energy to significantly remain in the system. Therefore, temperature differences between night and day would be exceptionally large. The day would heat up dramatically (there would be no atmospheric buffer to *prevent* a large influx of solar radiation into the system) and the night would be *very* cold (there would be no atmosphere to keep any of the heat in the system). See Questions 2 and 3 below for further discussion.

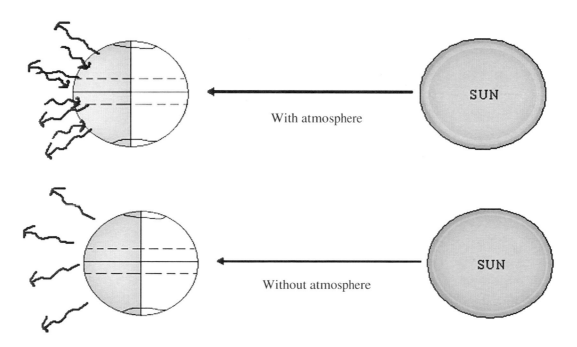

With atmosphere

Without atmosphere

2. At what hour is the hottest time of day? At what hour is the coolest time of day?

This question follows from Question #1 above. Throughout the day, solar radiation is being absorbed by the Earth system. Remember, however, that some of that incoming solar radiation is being absorbed by the ground, radiated upward, absorbed by the atmosphere, and then radiated back down to the surface of the Earth. In the process, some of the energy (visible radiation) will not be absorbed by the surface of the Earth, but rather be reflected off the surface of the Earth back through the atmosphere and into space. As long as there is a greater amount of energy being *absorbed* by the surface (and then radiated back to the atmosphere in the form of heat radiation – thermal infrared) than being reflected off the surface, the day will continue to heat up. Greater amounts of reflection typically occurs when the Sun is low in the sky. Therefore, the day will continue to heat up right until around 3 to 4 p.m. After 4 p.m. the low Sun produces more reflection of sunlight on the ground versus absorption of sunlight by the ground. See Question #4 below for further discussion. Also, see Table 1 from Question #9 below for a description of *albedo*.

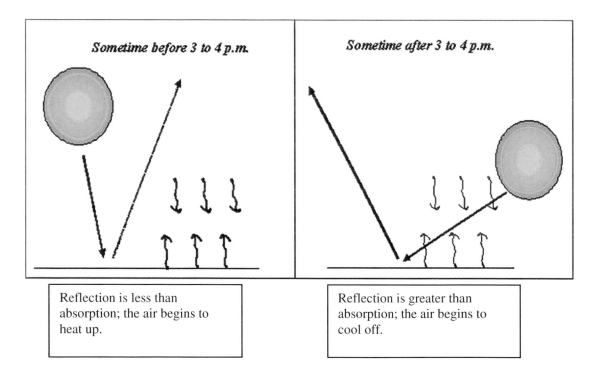

The coolest time of day will occur when the atmosphere has lost as much heat energy as it possible can. Heat energy is lost throughout the entire evening (there is no solar energy to provide energy to the surface or the atmosphere). Until the Sun rises, therefore, the day will get colder and colder. Sun rises at dawn. Therefore, the coldest time of day will be directly after dawn. Shortly after dawn, the surface and the atmosphere begin once again to absorb solar energy at a quicker rate than it loses solar energy. The heating process will begin anew.

3. Which is hotter, Mercury or Venus? Why?

This question is included to emphasize the importance of atmosphere. Although Mercury is the closest planet to the Sun (Venus is second closest), Venus is still the hottest planet in the solar system. Why? Venus has a very thick carbon dioxide atmosphere. Carbon dioxide is a greenhouse gas. Greenhouse gases absorb heat energy and radiate it back down toward the surface. On Venus, *visible* solar radiation enters into the system and then gets absorbed by the surface of Venus. The absorbed energy then radiates upward in the form of thermal infrared radiation (TIR = heat). The thick carbon dioxide atmosphere then absorbs this energy and eventually radiates it back toward the surface. Because Venus has such a thick carbon dioxide atmosphere, little to no heat energy can escape. Venus has what is called a "runaway greenhouse effect". Mercury has a very thin sodium atmosphere. The atmosphere is not thick enough to retain any heat, so the nighttime side of Mercury is actually *very* cold.

Venus data: Average surface temperature   = 457°C = 855°F

Mercury data: surface temperature   = -173°C = -279°F (nighttime side)
      = 427°C = 800°F (daytime side)

4. What is the primary source of heat for the troposphere; that is, how does the troposphere heat up?

Three primary wavelengths of solar radiation enter into the Earth's atmosphere: Ultraviolet (UV), Thermal Infrared (TIR), and Visible (V). The majority of UV rays are absorbed by the ozone layer found within the stratosphere (see Question #1 from Chapter 3). The majority of TIR rays are absorbed by greenhouse gases in the atmosphere (such as water vapor and carbon dioxide) and then radiated back out into space. A large quantity of V rays move directly through the atmosphere and then strike the surface of the Earth (although, another good portion of V rays are reflected and scattered by the atmosphere back into space). Of the V rays that make it to the surface of the Earth, some of them will reflect off of the surface back to the atmosphere, and then eventually back into space; whereas some of the V rays will get absorbed in the surface. When V rays are absorbed in the surface, the surface will then heat up and begin to emit TIR. In other words, the ground is getting hot from the absorption of V rays. The TIR rays now enter into the troposphere. Within the troposphere are greenhouse gases (such as carbon dioxide, water vapor, and methane) that absorb the TIR rays and radiate them back to the surface of the Earth. Thus, the troposphere is being heated from the surface to the sky (or, from the bottom up). In addition, the heated ground is in contact with air. The air heats up via *conduction* and mixes the warm air with cold air found above via *convection* (see Question #5, Chapter 7). See diagram below:

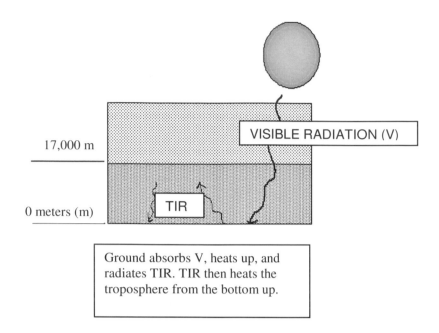

17,000 m

VISIBLE RADIATION (V)

0 meters (m)

TIR

Ground absorbs V, heats up, and
radiates TIR. TIR then heats the
troposphere from the bottom up.

5. Mountaintops are closer to the Sun than are lowlands, and yet mountaintops are typically colder than lowlands. Why?

The atmosphere acts as a "blanket", keeping the heat in, keeping us warm. Recall Question #4 above. The troposphere is being heated from the bottom up. In the end, atmospheric heating represents the majority of the heat that we feel. Therefore, the thicker the atmosphere, the greater the amount of trapped heat. As we move from low elevations to high elevations, the density of the atmosphere is decreasing (please see Question #2, Chapter 3). Therefore, it is reasonable to suggest that lower elevations will be warmer than higher elevations. Simply put, there is a thicker atmospheric blanket at low elevations versus at higher elevations. This does not mean that it will *never* be warm (or even hot) at high elevations. The thin air of higher elevations is able to absorb and reflect out *less* amounts of incoming solar radiation than lower elevations. Therefore, high warmth levels at upper elevations can (and do) occur.

6. The environmental lapse rate (ELR) is 6.5°C/1000 meters. If the surface temp is 25°C (77°F), what is the air temp at 10,000 meters (32,800 feet) above sea level?

The ELR is the average rate of temperature change as one moves through the atmosphere. As we know from Question #5 above, the atmosphere gets cooler and cooler (on average) with an increase in elevation due to the air becoming thinner. We can approximate this temperature change using the ELR:

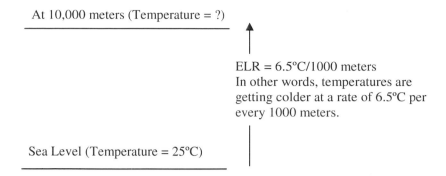

Change of elevation = 0 meters to 10,000 meters = 10,000 meters. So,

(6.5°C/1000 meters) x (10,000 meters) = 65°C (or, 10,000 meters elevation is 65°C = 149°F colder than at sea level). Therefore, the temperature at 10,000 meters is 25°C - 65°C = -40°C.

7. The dry adiabatic lapse rate (DALR) is 10°C/1000 meters. The wet adiabatic lapse rate (WALR) is 5°C/1000 meters. The equation for the lifting condensation level (LCL) is (T − T$_{DEW}$) x 1000/8. Assume air is flowing across and then up a mountain. Using the following data calculate: a) Height of the LCL; b) Temperature at the LCL; c) Temperature at the summit of the mountain (assume the mountain has a 5000 meter summit); and d) Temperature at the surface of the leeward side of the mountain. Note: T at sea level = 40°C. T$_{DEW}$ = 16°C.

In this question, "dry" air is air that has a relative humidity of less than 100%; "wet" air is air that has a relative humidity of equal to or greater than 100%. Dry air and wet air, upon upward movement through the atmosphere, change temperature at different rates.

As air moves upward, it expands. Upon expansion, air molecules in the mass of air move apart from one another and therefore less molecular collisions will occur. Because of the lesser number of molecular collisions, the air will get cooler and cooler (i.e., there is a decrease in the rate of energy exchange between molecules). This type of cooling process is called "adiabatic" because heat is not being removed to or added from the system; nevertheless, the temperature of the air mass is still decreasing:

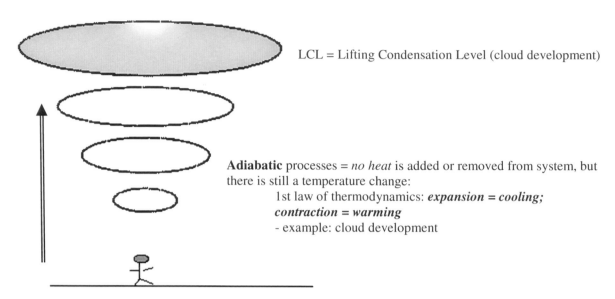

LCL = Lifting Condensation Level (cloud development)

Adiabatic processes = *no heat* is added or removed from system, but there is still a temperature change:
       1st law of thermodynamics: ***expansion = cooling;***
       contraction = warming
       - example: cloud development

As the parcel of air rises, it expands. As it expands it cools. When the air reaches the LCL it has dropped to the dew point temperature. Now, the relative humidity of the air is 100%. Water vapor in the air now condenses to liquid water (i.e., a cloud will form).

The LCL (Lifting Condensation Level) is the point where the air has cooled to the "dew point" temperature. The dew point temperature is the temperature at which Relative Humidity (RH) equals 100% (see next chapter for questions regarding dew point and humidity).

Like most questions that involve some type of "visual" mathematical problem, it is always best to draw the picture. The large arrow in the drawing below indicates the direction of air flow ("windward" is the side of the mountain facing the wind; "leeward" is the side of the mountain opposite the wind):

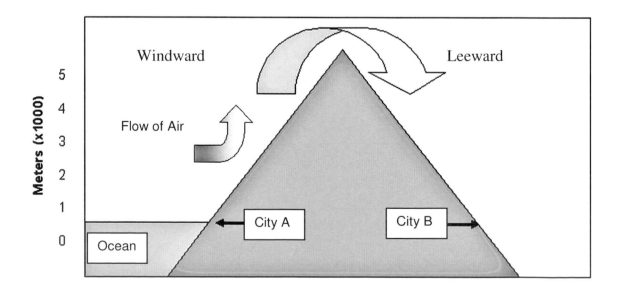

a) What is the height of the LCL?

$LCL = (T - T_{DEW}) \times 1000/8$

T = temperature at sea level = 40°C (104°F)
T_{DEW} = dew point temperature = 16°C (61°F)

So, LCL   = (40°C - 16°C) x 1000/8
                 = 24°C x 1000/8
                 = 3 x 1000
                 = 3000 meters

b) What is the temperature at the LCL?

The temperature at the LCL is simply the dew point temperature = 16°C

c) What is the temperature at the summit of the mountain?

The summit is at 5000 meters. The temperature at 3000 meters (LCL) is 16°C. The difference in height between the summit and the LCL is 5000 meters − 3000 meters = 2000 meters. Remember, that at and above the LCL, the RH is greater than or equal to 100%. Therefore, as the air continues to rise upward from the LCL it will continue to cool off at the WALR (wet adiabatic lapse rate) = 5°C/1000 meters:

2000 meters x (5°C/1000 meters) = 10°C (50°F).

Therefore, the summit is 10°C cooler than the LCL:

T at LCL = 16°C (61°F)

So, T at summit = 16°C - 10°C = 6°C (43°F)

d) What is the temperature at the surface of the leeward side of the mountain (City B in the diagram above)?

The height difference between the summit and City B is 5000 meters. Now, because the air is flowing downward, it is going to *heat* up rather than cool off (the molecules in the air are becoming tightly packed and more molecular collisions will occur). Now, although the air at the summit has an RH of greater than or equal to 100%, it will *not* heat up according to the WALR (on its way down the summit). As a matter of fact, as long as the air is being forced *downward* it will heat up according to the DALR (Dry Adiabatic Lapse Rate) = 10°C/1000 meters:

Distance from summit to city B = 5000 meters

DALR = 10°C/1000 meters. Thus,

5000 meters x (10°C/1000 meters) = 50°C (122°F)

Therefore, the temperature at City B is 50°C warmer than at the summit:

City B = 6°C (temperature at summit) + 50°C = 56°C (133°F)

An interesting note: Although City A and City B are at the same elevation (sea level), City A has a temperature of 40°C and City B has a temperature of 56°C; that's a 16°C (61°F) change in temperature! This question reveals the mountains ability to create a "rainshadow" effect.

8. How does the temperature regime of a densely wooded location differ from that of a nearby un-forested location?

During the night, heat is still radiating from the surface (see Question #4 above). For the densely wooded location, much of that radiating heat will be absorbed by the trees and then radiated back to the surface. For the un-forested location, most of the heat radiation will flow upward through the atmosphere and eventually lost to space. Therefore, at night, the wooded location will generally be warmer than the un-forested location. What about during the day? During the day two things are occurring which will make the forested location a *cooler* place than the un-forested location. First (and most obvious), the forested site will block a lot of incoming solar radiation. Shadows will be prevalent and temperatures will be cooler. At the un-forested site, there will be no blocking of incoming solar radiation. Therefore, a lot of radiation will be absorbed by the surface and will subsequently cause surface heating (which, in turn, will heat the air). The other reason why the forested site will be a cooler place during the day is *latent heat of evaporation*. Plants undergo *evapotranspiration*. During a plants physiologic cycle, moisture is released from tiny pores on the leaf tissue called *stomata* (see Question #4, Chapter 9). As the water is released from the surface of the plant, heat from the surrounding air evaporates the water (this entire process is *evapotranspiration*). Subsequently, the air temperature surrounding the plant decreases. Because of evapotranspiration, grassy, forested, or simply marine environments tend to be cooler than non-vegetated or dry areas. This is one of the reasons why rural areas are cooler than suburban areas. So, where has all the heat gone? The heat from the surrounding air is absorbed in the water! Note: during the phase change of liquid to vapor (evaporation), the temperature of the water *does not* change (this is a *latent heat* process). Water has an ability to store heat within its molecular structure. In the end, the evaporated water (which is lighter than the surrounding air) rises in the sky and moves to another location. Therefore, not only will the forested site be cooler during the day due to shadowing, it will also be cooler due to latent heat of evaporation.

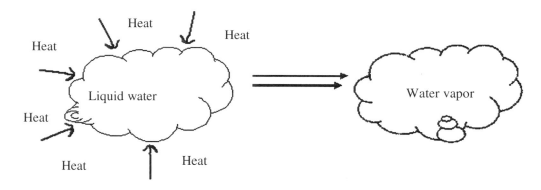

Bonus Question: Why do you cool off when you sweat?

Answer: As we sweat, water accumulates on our skin. As this water absorbs the heat from the surrounding air, the water will evaporate. As the water evaporates, the air temperature will subsequently decrease (heat is being removed the air and trapped within the water vapor molecule). So, the reason we cool off when we sweat is principally because the air *surrounding* our body loses heat during the sweat evaporation process.

9. How is albedo a factor in your selection of outdoor clothing on a hot, sunny day? What about on a cold, clear, winter day?

Albedo refers to reflectivity. Surfaces with high albedo have a high reflectivity, and will subsequently reflect a large proportion of incoming solar radiation. Surfaces with a low albedo have a low reflectivity, and will subsequently absorb a large proportion of incoming solar radiation. Table 1 below indicates the average albedo of various surfaces.

Table 1
Selected Albedo Values of Various Surfaces

Surface	Albedo (% Reflected)
Fresh Snow	80 – 95%
Polluted or old snow	40 – 70%
Ocean (Sun near horizon)	40%
Ocean (afternoon Sun)	5%
Coniferous forest	10 – 15%
Deciduous forest (green)	15 – 20%
Crops (green)	10 – 25%
Bare, dry sandy soil	25 – 45%
Bare, dark soil	5 – 15%
White sand	40%
Desert	25 – 30%
Meadow, grass	15 – 25%
Concrete (sidewalk)	20 – 30%
Asphalt (parking lot)	5 – 10%

Therefore, on a hot, sunny day you would be wise to wear light colors. Light colored clothing has a high albedo and will therefore reflect a lot of incoming solar radiation. On a cold, clear, winter day you would be wise to wear dark colors. Dark colored clothing has a low albedo and will therefore absorb a lot of incoming solar radiation thus keeping you warmer.

What if the cold day was not clear but was cloudy?

What if it was a cold evening not a cold day?

Chapter 5: Atmospheric Moisture

1. If a parcel of air at 30°C has an absolute humidity of 40 millibars, what is the parcel's relative humidity?

Next to temperature and pressure, the most common piece of information in local weather broadcasts is *relative humidity*. Relative humidity (RH) is the amount of water vapor in the air divided by the total amount of water vapor that can exist in the air (at a given temperature) before the air is completely saturated:

RH =   (actual water vapor *content* in air)   x 100
        (water vapor *capacity* of the air)

The proportion of air that is made up of water vapor molecules is termed *water vapor pressure* and is expressed in units of millibars (mb). The *maximum* water vapor pressure capacity of air is expressed as *saturation vapor pressure* (SVP). SVP represents the maximum amount of water vapor that the air can "hold" before the air is saturated.

If the water vapor pressure equals the SVP, then RH – 100% (the temperature at which RH = 100% is known as the *dew point* temperature). This means that the air cannot "hold" any more water vapor. If any more water vapor is added to the air, the vapor will immediately *condense* out as liquid water. Also, if one were to decrease the air temperature of saturated air, condensation will occur.

Warmer air has a greater ability to "hold" water vapor than cooler air. Warm air has more energy than cool air, therefore warm air can produce higher rates of evaporation than cool air (meaning, there are more molecular collisions in warm air than cool air). Therefore, the warmer air "holds" *more* amounts of water vapor before the water vapor condenses (there is enough energy to keep evaporation high.). See graph below.

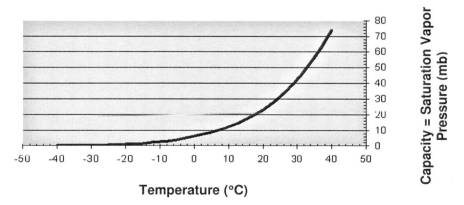

As noted above, in order to change relative humidity, one can either alter the *content* of moisture in the sky, or, simply alter the temperature. By changing the temperature, you effectively change the *capacity* of air to "hold" moisture ("moisture" being water vapor). Therefore, air temperature and capacity become interchangeable.

In order to answer the above question, we must first determine what the capacity is. Using the graph above, we note that if the air temperature is 30°C then its *capacity* is 42 mb. *Content* (also known as *absolute humidity*) is given in the question as 40 mb. Therefore, in order to calculate the relative humidity we simply use the following equation:

$$RH = \frac{(\text{actual water vapor } \textit{content} \text{ in air})}{(\text{water vapor } \textit{capacity} \text{ of the air})} \times 100 = \frac{40 \text{ mb}}{42 \text{ mb}} \times 100 = 95\%$$

2. A parcel of air at 40°C has a relative humidity of 50%. What is the parcel's dew point temperature?

We know that dew point temperature is the temperature at which relative humidity = 100% (or, the temperature at which the air is saturated). If the relative humidity = 100%, then the *content* and the *capacity* will be equal. Remember the following equation:

$$RH = \frac{(\text{actual water vapor } \textit{content} \text{ in air})}{(\text{water vapor } \textit{capacity} \text{ of the air})} \times 100$$

If we rearrange the equation, we can solve for *content*:

$$\text{Content} = \frac{(RH) \times \text{capacity}}{100}$$

Using the graph from the question above, we note that the *capacity* of air at a temperature of 40°C is 74 millibar (mb). Thus,

$$\text{Content} = \frac{50\% \times 74 \text{ mb}}{100} = 37 \text{ mb}$$

Remember, in order for RH to be 100%, content *must equal* capacity. In other words, we need to decrease the temperature to such a level that the capacity will change from 74 mb to 37 mb. Therefore, using the graph from the previous question, all we need to do is look up the temperature of air that has a capacity of 37 mb: ***Answer:*** In order to achieve saturation, the air temperature must decrease to 27°C = dew point temperature.

3. How is it possible to have an air mass over the hot, dry Sahara desert contain twice as much moisture as air over the cool, wet Quebec, Canada region?

From Questions #1 and #2 above, we know that relative humidity is dependent upon both the *content* of moisture in the air and the temperature of the air (which effects *capacity*). We also know that as temperature increases, capacity increases, which means relative humidity will decrease:

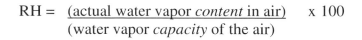

$$RH = \frac{(\text{actual water vapor } \textit{content} \text{ in air})}{(\text{water vapor } \textit{capacity} \text{ of the air})} \times 100$$

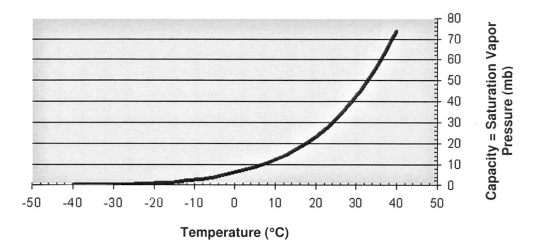

Temperature (°C)

Although the Sahara (at times) has more content than Quebec, due to the high temperatures of the Sahara the *capacity* of air is very high (thus, producing a low relative humidity). When Quebec is cool, the capacity in Quebec is low, thereby *increasing* its relative humidity. In other words, the standard to compare moisture throughout the world is neither content nor capacity. Rather it is relative humidity which considers both variables.

4. What makes Death Valley one of the hottest and driest places on the planet?

We can refer to Question #7 of Chapter 4 to help us here. As air moves upward it expands and cools off according to the adiabatic lapse rate (*adiabatic* means that neither heat is added to or removed from a system, nevertheless a temperature change still occurs). As air rises and expands, it will drop in temperature according to the dry adiabatic lapse rate (DALR) or the wet adiabatic lapse rate (WALR) dependent upon the humidity (if the air is saturated, i.e., relative humidity is equal to or greater than 100%, it will cool off according to the WALR). When the air moves downward, it will contract and heat up according to the DALR *regardless* of the humidity of the air. If we refer to Question #7 of Chapter 4, we note that City B on the leeward side of the mountain is a good 16°C warmer than City A on the windward side of the mountain. Remember, as temperature increases, the capacity of air to "hold" moisture increases. Therefore, relative humidity will *decrease* (see Question #3 above). Therefore, not only is the adiabatic process creating warmer air (at City B), but also drier air. Death Valley is located on the leeward side of the Sierra Nevada Mountains – 200 feet *below* sea level! Air, as it flows down the leeward side of the Sierra Nevada's will both heat up and dry off at an extraordinary rate:

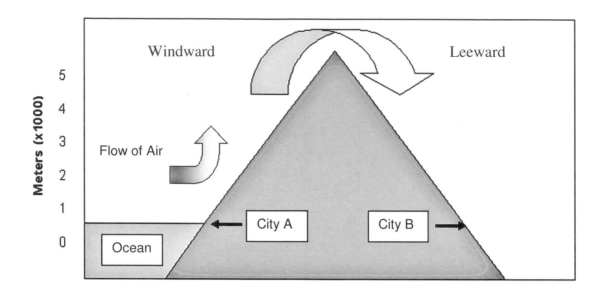

5. From the prior chapter, you determined why you cool off when you sweat. With this in mind, answer the following question: Which is generally more comfortable to be in, "dry" heat or "wet" heat?

Recall that you cool off when you sweat due to water on your skin evaporating. The water evaporates because heat from the surrounding air is absorbed in the water molecule. The evaporated water then floats away, taking with it heat from the surrounding air. The surrounding air, which lost heat, drops in temperature. Subsequently, you cool off. Now, if air is "dry", then relative humidity is low. If humidity is low, then rates of evaporation can be quite high. Therefore, any water on your skin will evaporate quickly and you will feel cool faster. If air is "wet", on the other hand, then relative humidity is high. If humidity is high, then rates of evaporation will be quite slow (the air is already "full" with moisture). Therefore, any water on your skin will not be able to evaporate quickly and you will feel both warm and sticky. Therefore, most people are more comfortable in dry heat rather than wet heat.

6. Imagine that you are deciding when, in your daily schedule, to water the garden. What time of day would be best for conserving water? Why?

Remember (see Questions #1 to 4 above) the capacity of air to "hold" moisture *increases* when the air temperature increases. Also remember that as the capacity increases, relative humidity (RH) can decrease (note the inverse relationship between RH and capacity):

RH = (actual water vapor *content* in air)   x 100
       (water vapor *capacity* of the air)

During the course of the day, the air temperature continues to rise until about 3 to 4 pm (for the reason why, see Question #2 from Chapter 4). Therefore, during the course of the day (if the content of moisture remains the same), RH will drop as the temperature increases (remember, capacity is increasing). Now, recall that if the air is "dry", rates of evaporation will be high (see Question # 5 above). So, during the course of the day: 1) air temperature increases, 2) water vapor capacity increases, and 3) RH decreases. Low RH means that the air is drier, which means that rates of evaporation will be high (in other words, liquid water will evaporate relatively quickly). Now, if you want to water your garden, you want to water it at a time when rates of evaporation will be low, not high (you don't want all the liquid water to evaporate away!). The best time to water the garden, therefore, is when the air temperature is cool not warm. Hence the best time to water the garden is in the early morning or late evening when air temperatures are lower.

7. Why do the windows of your car get foggy on cold days (or, cold evenings)?

As noted from the previous questions, as air temperature increases, water vapor capacity increases, and RH decreases. Conversely, if air temperature decreases, water vapor capacity decreases, and RH increases.

Now, as air temperature decreases (and as water vapor capacity decreases), the RH will continue to increase. The temperature at which RH is 100% is called the "dew point temperature" (see Questions #1 and 2 above). When the dew point temperature is reached, the rate of evaporation will equal the rate of condensation, and water droplets can now develop (this, by the way, is how fog develops). Study the following two images:

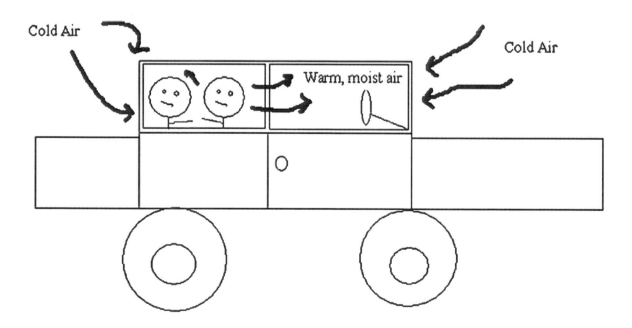

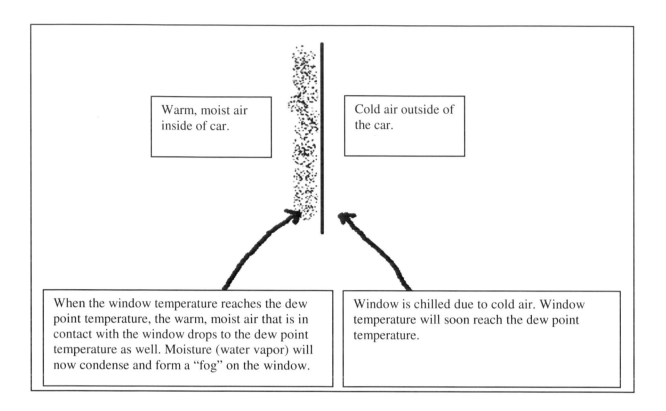

Warm, moist air inside of car.

Cold air outside of the car.

When the window temperature reaches the dew point temperature, the warm, moist air that is in contact with the window drops to the dew point temperature as well. Moisture (water vapor) will now condense and form a "fog" on the window.

Window is chilled due to cold air. Window temperature will soon reach the dew point temperature.

Chapter 6: Atmospheric Pressure

1. Atmospheric pressure *decreases* at the rate of 0.036 millibars (mb) per foot as one ascends through the lower portion of the atmosphere. The Sears Tower in Chicago, Illinois is one of the world's tallest buildings at 1450 feet. If the street-level pressure is 1020.4 mb, what is the air pressure at the top of the Sears Tower?

As one travels higher into the atmosphere, air pressure *decreases* due to the fact that there is less air mass at higher elevations (see Question #2, Chapter 3). Remember, air pressure is simply just the mass of air multiplied by gravity:

Air Pressure (weight of atmosphere) = (mass of air) X (gravity)

Gravity is the seemingly invisible force that keeps everything secured to Earth. For example, if you jumped out of an airplane, or, if you simply fell out of your bed you would fall back to Earth at a rate of = 9.8 meters/sec^2 = 32 feet/sec^2 (this means that for every second you fall, your speed of descent will increase by 32 feet/sec). Gravity does not change significantly from place to place across Earth. What can change significantly, however, is the mass of air at any given location. The differences in air mass from place to place is *one* of the reasons why there are different air pressures across the globe, and hence one reason for wind and other weather dynamics (air flows from high pressure to low pressure).

The rate of air pressure change of 0.036 millibars (mb) per foot of elevation is an approximation that will differ with environmental conditions. Nevertheless, it is a good physical estimate (based upon volume and density calculations) that generally works well.

Change = 1450 ft x 0.036 mb/ft = 52.2 mb

Air pressure at top of building =

1020.4 mb – 52.2 mb = 968.2 mb

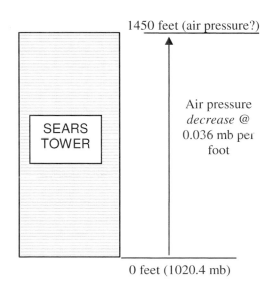

1450 feet (air pressure?)

Air pressure *decrease* @ 0.036 mb per foot

0 feet (1020.4 mb)

2. Water boils at 100°C (212°F) and freezes at 0°C (32°F) at sea level. At higher elevations (where atmospheric pressure is less than at sea level), will water boil at a higher or lower temperature than at sea level? Will ice melt at a higher or lower temperature? Why?

The answer is that water will boil at a temperature *lower* than 100°C and melt at a temperature *higher* than 0°C at elevation. Remember, at higher elevations air pressure is lower than at lower elevations (the quantity of air at high elevations is less than at lower elevations). So, why does ice melt more easily with higher pressure (at low elevations) while water boils more easily with lower pressure (at high elevations)? Simply put, during the process of ice melting into water the volume of the ice *decreases*. With added pressure there is additional pressure on the ice thus aiding the volume-decrease process. In other words, the melt temperature can be lower if the pressure is increased. Remember, ice typically melts at temperatures that are above the freezing point (0°C). At high elevations ice melts at temperatures higher than 0°C, but at lower elevations the ice melts at temperatures *less* than 0°C.

During the boiling (or evaporation process) the volume of water *increases*. The removal of pressure (at higher elevations) aids in the expansion process thereby increasing rates of evaporation (so, for example, at 10,000 feet elevation water will boil at 90°C rather than 100°C; at -200 feet elevation water will boil at a temperature greater than 100°C.)

3. A baseball pitcher pitching at sea level goes to Coors Field in Denver, Colorado to pitch for the Colorado Rockies. What is the biggest problem (adjustment) the pitcher must face?

When the Colorado Rockies were born a number of years ago, many baseball fans suggested that the Rockies had an unfair advantage playing at Coors Field. Coors Field is at an altitude of about 1 mile. At this altitude the air is thinner and the air pressure is less than at sea level (see Question #2, Chapter 3; and Question #1 above). Because of this, there will be less air friction on the ball when it soars through the sky, hence the ball is able to travel farther than it would at sea level (this is why we see games such as 10 runs to 15 at Coors Field!). But, why would the Rockies have an unfair advantage? Certainly, opposing teams playing at Coors Field also reap the benefits of the thin air and therefore should be able to hit more homeruns too, yes? So, how do the Rockies have an unfair advantage?

One of the toughest pitches to hit in baseball is the "breaking" pitch, or, curveball. The pitch is so named because as the pitcher releases the ball, it curves through the air on the way to the batter. If the pitcher can get the ball to curve at just the right time the batter will swing and miss. How does the pitcher curve the ball? When the pitcher releases the ball he spins the ball with a flick of the wrist and fingers. The curve, therefore, is dependent upon the ability of the pitcher to spin the ball coupled with the amount of air in the sky. In other words, the greater the density of air, the greater the air friction on the ball and hence the easier it is for the ball to curve. Ah! This is the dilemma. At Coors Field, the air is thinner than at sea level, therefore it is more difficult to "break" the ball. Pitcher's for the Colorado Rockies are able to practice in the thin air and therefore learn how to spin the ball in such a way as to curve the ball even in the thin air (see diagram below). Opposing pitchers, on the other hand, come into Coors Field with less of an ability to curve the ball; hence the advantage goes to the Colorado Rockies. During the first few seasons of the Rockies, we saw them win many games. Since then, however, the Rockies have not done so well. As it turns out, it takes a tremendous amount of torque in the pitcher's shoulder to spin the ball adequately at Coors Field. Pitchers that pitch at this high altitude for any length of time hurt their shoulders quicker (and have a shortened baseball career). Needless to say, it has been difficult for the Colorado Rockies to maintain a good pitching staff!

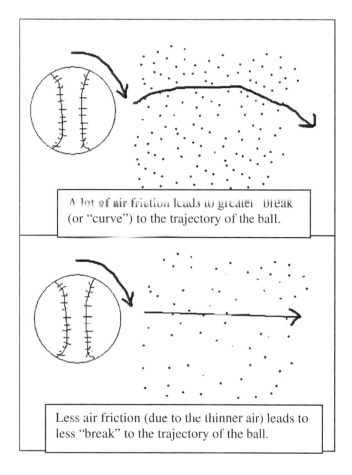

A lot of air friction leads to greater "break" (or "curve") to the trajectory of the ball.

Less air friction (due to the thinner air) leads to less "break" to the trajectory of the ball.

4. What will eventually happen to a helium balloon as it goes higher and higher into the atmosphere? *Bonus Question:* What will happen to a deep sea creature if you quickly bring it to the surface?

Air pressure at sea level is 14.7 lbs/in^2 (or, about 1013 millibars). In other words, if you are at sea level, on every square inch of your body there will be about 14.7 pounds of air pressure pushing in on you. So, why don't we all just implode due to the enormous pressure of air? We don't implode because our bodies are in a state of equilibrium with our environment. In other words, while it's true that you have 14.7 lbs/in^2 pushing in on you, your internal body pressure is also pushing outward at the same 14.7 lbs/in^2. Equilibrium. What about the balloon?

Helium is a gas that weighs less than oxygen and nitrogen (the primary components of the atmosphere). Therefore, helium is buoyant in the air and floats upward (this is why a helium balloon will rise upward whereas a balloon that you blow up with your breath will not). Now, let's say that you have a helium balloon and you are at sea level. The balloon is in equilibrium; that is, the balloon is neither expanding nor contracting due to the fact that there is equal pressure pushing on the balloon and out from the balloon (the helium molecules bouncing around inside the balloon create a pressure). So, at sea level, the pressures inside the balloon and outside the balloon are 14.7 lbs/in^2. When you release the balloon, as it lifts into the sky, the internal pressure remains 14.7 lbs/in^2 throughout its journey, but remember (see Question #1 above) as you go higher into the atmosphere the density of air decreases therefore air pressure pushing on the balloon *decreases* as well. The result: the balloon will continually expand until the density of the "air" inside the balloon equals the density of air outside of the balloon. When this happens the balloon will stop rising and simply move with the air currents (eventually, the helium will escape through the balloon membrane and fall back to the surface of the Earth).

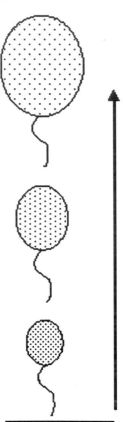

Bonus Question: What will happen to a *deep* sea creature if you quickly bring it to the surface?

Answer: It will explode! Why?

Chapter 7: Atmospheric and Oceanic Circulation

1. If you were to camp on a steep mountain slope at night where would your tent site best be located (relative to a large smoky campfire) – Hint: you DO NOT want to get smoked by the fire?

The big concepts in this question are heat and density. During the night air temperature begins to decrease on the mountain. At the base of the mountain the air temperature drops but not as quickly as near the top of the mountain. At the top of the mountain, there is less air (see Question #2, Chapter 3), therefore heat can escape through the atmosphere (and eventually into space) quicker (see Questions #4 and 5, Chapter 4). Now, cold air is more compact relative to warm air, therefore the colder air at the top of the mountain will be heavier than the air at the base of the mountain. Heavier air will sink, thereby producing a flow of air coming from the top of the mountain toward the base of the mountain. This type of air flow is known as a *mountain breeze*. Therefore, if you don't want to get smoked by your fire, you should pop your tent *upslope* of the camp fire:

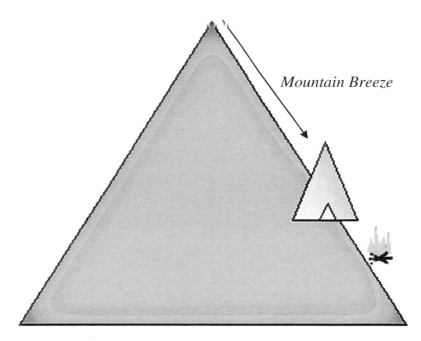

Mountain Breeze

2. When do you think a sea breeze would be the *strongest*, in the winter or the summer? Why?

As the name implies, a *sea breeze* is air that originates from the sea, heads toward the coast, and then eventually moves inland. A sea breeze forms due to air pressure differences on the sea versus the land (that is, a high pressure cell develops over the sea relative to a low pressure cell developing over land. Because air flows from high pressure toward low pressure, a wind will result). In order to answer the above question we must first understand what creates the pressure differences on sea and land. The concept we'll look into is called *specific heat.*

All things being equal, land and water change temperature according to their respective *specific heat.* Specific heat is the amount of heat needed to change the temperature of 1 gram of a substance by 1 degree Centigrade. Water has the highest specific heat of most substances. In other words, in order to dramatically increase the temperature of a quantity of water *a lot* of heat gain is needed. Similarly, in order to dramatically decrease the temperature of a quantity of water *a lot* of heat loss is needed. On the other hand, land has a relatively low specific heat (only a small amount of heat gain or heat loss is needed to dramatically change the temperature of a quantity of land). Hence, the reason for *hot* beach sand on a nice, sunny day). An example of specific heat: San Diego, CA and Tucson, Arizona are both at 32° N. Latitude. Because these two cities are at the same latitude one would expect similar temperature conditions throughout the year. However, during the summer months San Diego has an average temperature range of 70° to 80° Fahrenheit. Tucson has an average temperature range of 80° to 100°+ Fahrenheit. During the winter months San Diego has an average temperature range of 60° to 70° F. Tucson has an average temperature range of 40° to 50° F. As can be seen in this example, the high specific heat of San Diego's marine environment (in-part) moderates San Diego temperatures (keeping us cool in the summer and warm in the winter). Tucson on the other hand is continental (meaning a lower specific heat and greater temperature change).

Look at the diagram below. Because of the specific heat difference between land and water, the water remains relatively cool (even on a sunny day) compared to the beach sand.

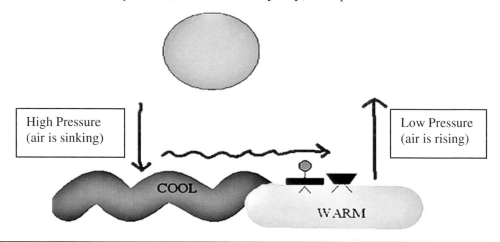

Air flows from high to low pressure (from the ocean to the land) creating the "seabreeze".

One of the ways to alter surface pressure is by changing the surface temperature. Although not a rule of thumb, surface heating can lead to the development of low pressure systems (as the ground heats up the air, the air expands, becomes less dense and floats upward. This leads to low pressure.) and surface cooling can lead to the development of a high pressure system (as the ground cools, the air contracts, becomes more dense and sinks. This leads to high pressure.). In the picture below the surface cooling of the ocean and the surface heating of the land create the pressure differences needed to begin the sea breeze

Now that we know what a sea breeze is and where it comes from, we can determine when a sea breeze will be the strongest. A sea breeze will be the strongest when the pressure differences between the water and the land are the highest. The pressure differences will be the highest when the temperature differences between the water and the land are the greatest. The temperature differences are the greatest during the *summer*; at this time, the beach sand will heat up dramatically relative to the water due to increased daylight hours and direct solar rays (the water won't heat up too much due to its very high specific heat).

3. If you flushed a toilet in Australia, in which direction would the toilet water turn?

This question was perhaps made most famous by the *Simpson's* cartoon (as Bart Simpson flushed the toilet in Australia...) and involves a concept called the *Coriolis Effect*. The Coriolis Effect is a rather weak "force" that effects the direction of all moving objects on planet Earth (wind, water currents, airplanes, migrating birds, missiles, etc.). All objects traveling in the northern hemisphere get veered to the right of initial motion; all objects traveling in the southern hemisphere get veered to the left of initial motion.

The Earth rotates on its axis *easterly (or counterclockwise)*, once every 24 hours. Because the circumference of Earth gets smaller with higher latitudes, *tangential* velocity is unique from north to south across the planet (*circumference* $= \pi x D$. So, *Velocity* $= (\pi x D/24)$:

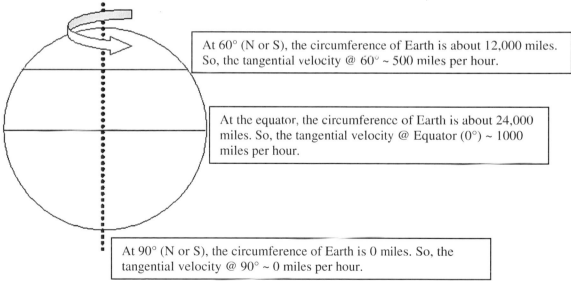

At 60° (N or S), the circumference of Earth is about 12,000 miles. So, the tangential velocity @ 60° ~ 500 miles per hour.

At the equator, the circumference of Earth is about 24,000 miles. So, the tangential velocity @ Equator (0°) ~ 1000 miles per hour.

At 90° (N or S), the circumference of Earth is 0 miles. So, the tangential velocity @ 90° ~ 0 miles per hour.

The differences in tangential velocity as noted in the above diagram leads to the Coriolis Effect. For example, let's say that a parcel of mail originating in Quito, Ecuador (located at 0° Latitude) is traveling due north toward Nova Scotia (via a very large sling-shot). Let us also say that the object is traveling at such a speed as to reach its destination in 1 hour.

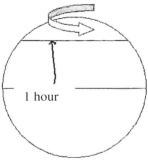

1 hour

Unfortunately, the folks sending the package did not take into consideration the Coriolis Effect. As a result, the package missed Nova Scotia to the right. Why? Remember, that at the Equator, the tangential velocity of motion is about 1000 mph. Because Earth rotates in a counterclockwise (or, easterly) direction, this tangential velocity component is directed toward the east. In other words, the package that left Ecuador was traveling to the north *and* to the east.

In the diagram below, the dotted line represents the "true path" that the object takes. Also remember that Nova Scotia is moving toward the east. At Nova Scotia (approximately, 60° N. Lat.) the tangential velocity is about 500 mph. So, after 1 hour of travel, the package has not only traveled to 60°N. Latitude, it has also traveled 1000 miles to the east. Nova Scotia has traveled only 500 miles to the east; the package has missed its destination by 500 miles:

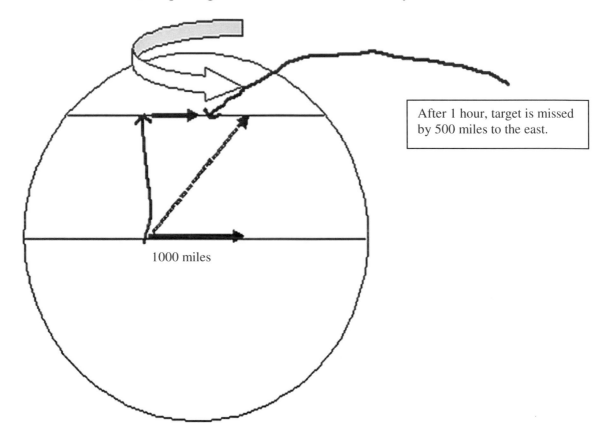

After 1 hour, target is missed by 500 miles to the east.

1000 miles

The Coriolis Effect is a weak "force". Only objects traveling long distances (such as wind and ocean currents) are noticeably affected by the Coriolis. Although a golf ball (and everything else "feels" the Coriolis), the force that you strike the golf ball with overwhelms any Coriolis force. So, what about the toilet? The toilet bowl is typically quite small. The directional force with which the water drops from the top of the bowl is much stronger than the Coriolis. Unless the toilet bowl has a "neutral" drop mechanism, you will see *no* Coriolis.

4. How does *decreasing* surface friction alter the Coriolis Effect on wind?

With decreased surface friction, winds will be faster. The Coriolis Effect is stronger for fast moving winds than for slow moving winds. Therefore, with less surface friction, the Coriolis Effect will be more evident. Where, therefore, will the strongest effects of the Coriolis be felt? *Answer*: Wind moving across ice sheets, oceans, empty desert plains, and the upper atmosphere where the winds are fast.

5. If solar radiation was distributed equally over the whole sky, what would happen to the Earth's atmosphere?

Remember, the Earth's atmosphere circulates because the Earth is unevenly heated; there is a surplus of solar energy at the Equator and a deficit of solar energy at the poles (surplus meaning there is more absorbed incoming solar radiation than there is energy flowing back to space; deficit meaning there is more energy flowing back to space than is being absorbed within the Earth system). The only reason why the equatorial regions don't fry and the polar regions don't freeze is due to *conduction*, *convection*, and *radiation*. Conduction, convection, and radiation are transport processes that move energy from surplus regions to deficit regions. Conduction transports energy through touch (usually through solids). Convection transports energy through mixing (usually through gas and liquids). Radiation transports energy through space.

In the pictures below, the stove top is sending heat to the bottom of the pot (via conduction); the heated water then migrates to the top of the pot displacing the cold water (via convection); the air above the water heats up and begins moving through the sky; additional heat is radiated from the stove top to the air. The end process is that warm gas or liquid moves toward cooler gas or liquid. Due to differential solar heating, the same effect is happening to our atmosphere. Therefore, uneven heating is a necessary component to our air and water circulation processes. If we had even distribution of heat, we would a world of stagnant air.

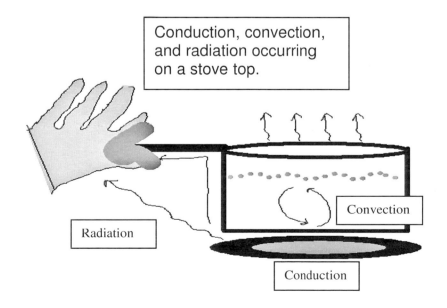

Conduction, convection, and radiation occurring on a stove top.

Radiation

Convection

Conduction

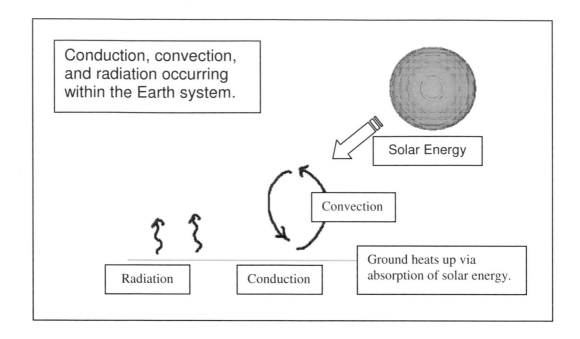

Part 3: Weather and Climate

Chapter 8: Air Mass Disturbances
Chapter 9: Global Climate Systems
Chapter 10: Paleoclimatology

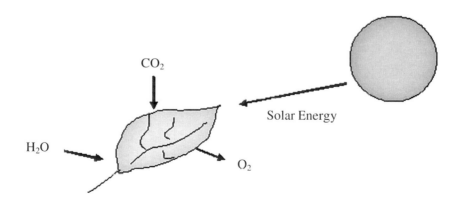

Chapter 8: Air Mass Disturbances

1. What continent is rarely threatened by hurricanes or cyclones? Why?

The map below shows the distribution of hurricanes, typhoons, and cyclones around the world (these storms are the same, just with different names; hurricanes occur in the Atlantic and East Pacific; typhoons occur in the West Pacific; cyclones occur in the Indian Ocean and Australia). The lower image shows the location of the 26°C (80°F) isotherm. In order for a hurricane to develop environmental conditions need to be met, with the most important condition being water temperature. Remember, a hurricane is an extremely large storm; rich in energy and water. In a hurricane, latent heat energy is bountiful within the water molecules. A hurricane needs a minimum water temperature of 26°C in order to feed and maintain itself with enough amounts of water vapor and energy. Water with temperature less than 26°C is too cold to "encourage" the growth of a hurricane (remember, warm water not only contains more energy than cold water, but warm water also evaporates easier than cold water, transporting the energy and moisture into the atmosphere quicker). Take a close look at the 26°C isotherm. You will notice that west of South America the water temperature is dominated with water that is less than 26°C (here, the coastline is getting feed by the cold Peruvian Current). East of South America, the quantity of water in excess of equal to 26°C is minimal (cold water currents travel up Africa and into the equatorial Atlantic toward South America). Because South America is not surrounded by water in excess of 26°C, the chances of a hurricane developing around South America are minimal. There just is not enough energy in the system to promote the development of a hurricane event.

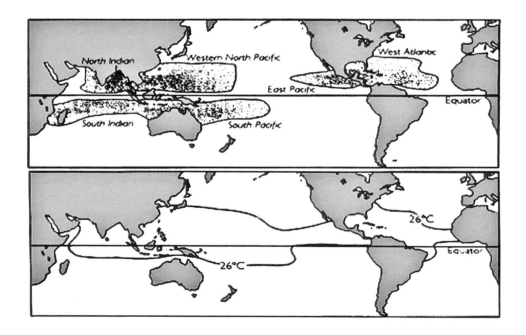

2. The Great Red Spot is a hurricane-like storm that has existed on Jupiter for over 300 years. In comparison, a hurricane on Earth will last about 1 to 2 weeks. Knowing what you know about hurricanes on Earth, what is so special about the surface of Jupiter?

Hurricanes on Earth develop over the tropical oceans where both warm water (see Question above) and latent heat are plentiful. In addition, surface friction over the oceans is minimal thus wind speeds exceed 75 miles per hour (a requirement for hurricanes). Hurricanes begin to dissipate when they hit land or when they travel across cold water. When they hit land, no longer is the storm over the source of energy (i.e., latent heat), nor is the storm over the source of matter (i.e., water). In addition, surface friction over the land is greater than the ocean, thus winds begin to slow down. If a hurricane travels from warm water to cold water, the source of latent heat energy drops dramatically and the storm begins to die down (see Question above).

With the above information, we can now draw some conclusions about the surface of Jupiter. Mind you, we need not know about Jupiter. We just need to know something about hurricanes on Earth. Based upon why a hurricane dissipates on Earth, we can assume the following: 1) Jupiter's surface is probably homogeneous (that is, the surface is the same nearly everywhere); and 2) there is a constant flow of energy from the surface into the Jovian (Jupiter's) atmosphere. Note, we did not say what the surface of Jupiter is made of nor did we comment on the temperature of the Jovian surface. Nevertheless, by knowing about hurricanes on Earth, we are able to draw some conclusions about the Great Red Spot and the surface of Jupiter.

3. Where is the safest place to be during a lightning event?

The safest place to be during a lightning event is the inside of a car, where the energy from the lightning can travel around the structure of the car, find its way to the tires, and then be grounded. However, while you are in the car, *do not* change the radio station at the time of the lightning strike! The energy can strike the radio antenna, travel through the wire system and then into your body. Note: contrary to popular belief, water is a rather *poor* conductor of electricity. Bathing in *distilled* (or, purified) water during a lightning event is relatively safe. However, non-purified water contains salts (ions) and other "impurities" which makes water an extremely *good* conductor of electricity. So, unless you are swimming in distilled water, stay away from bodies of water during a lightning event!

4. When you look at a cloud you are looking at droplets of water. Why don't these droplets of water *quickly* fall to the ground? When they do fall, what falls faster, a large raindrop or a small raindrop? Why?

Some historians suggest that Galileo Galilei (in the late sixteenth century) dropped two objects – a light one and a heavy one – off the Leaning Tower of Pisa. Galileo wanted to see which (if either object) would hit the ground first. He hypothesized that both objects, being subject to the same gravitational acceleration, would hit the ground at nearly the same time. He was correct. To a certain extent, however, Galileo's demonstration is counter-intuitive; a small bug would certainly take longer to fall from the top of a tall building than a bowling ball, wouldn't it? But what if you dropped both the bug and the bowling ball off of a tall building on the Moon? Which would hit the ground first? Galileo's experiment also seems to be at odds with the claim that small droplets of water will fall to the ground *slower* than large droplets of water. But they will. The solution must be that there is another force acting on the falling object besides gravity. Because Earth has an atmosphere, wind resistance (or, "drag) is also going to effect falling objects. The examination of these two forces (gravity and drag), will offer insight into why cloud droplets generally *don't* fall from the sky when they are small and why (when they are big enough to fall), the big ones fall *faster* than the small ones.

Force of Gravity is directly proportional to mass. For a droplet containing nothing but water molecules, mass is density times volume:

F_g = Force of Gravity = density x volume

Volume of a sphere = (4/3) x π x R^3 (where R = the radius of the sphere).

As the formula above indicates, the Force of Gravity is proportional to the *size* (radius) of the droplet.

Now, the drag (air resistance) between the droplet and the surrounding air depends on the velocity of fall and on the size of the droplet; the bigger the droplet then the more surface area in contact with air and the greater the air resistance. In addition, the faster the falling droplet, the more air resistance on the droplet:

F_d = Force of Drag ~ (velocity)^2 x surface area (size)

Surface area of a sphere = 4 x π x R^2

As the formula above indicates, the Force of Drag is also proportional to the size (radius) of the droplet. Now, as an object falls through the sky, eventually the Force of Gravity will equal the Force of Drag. When this happens the object will be falling at its "terminal velocity" and will no longer accelerate (that is, no longer increase in speed as it falls):

$F_g = F_d$

(density) x (4/3) x π x R^3 = (velocity)^2 x 4 x π x R^2

To find terminal velocity, we solve the above equation for velocity:

$$(velocity)^2 = \frac{(density) \times (4/3) \times \pi \times R^3}{4 \times \pi \times R^2}$$

So, velocity ~ square root of R. Simply put, as the radius of the droplet increases, there is a proportional *increase* in terminal velocity. Because large droplets (large radius) have a faster terminal velocity than small droplets (small radius), large droplets will reach the ground *faster* than small droplets. Conversely, the equation also states that a *strong updraft* of wind is needed to keep a large droplet in the sky whereas only a *slow updraft* of wind is needed to keep a small droplet in the sky (hence, the reason why water from clouds generally stays suspended). Thus, in order for Galileo's objects to have fallen at significantly different rates (and strike the ground at different times), the objects would needed to have been either *greatly* different in *size*, or, have fallen enough distance to have actually reached their terminal velocities.

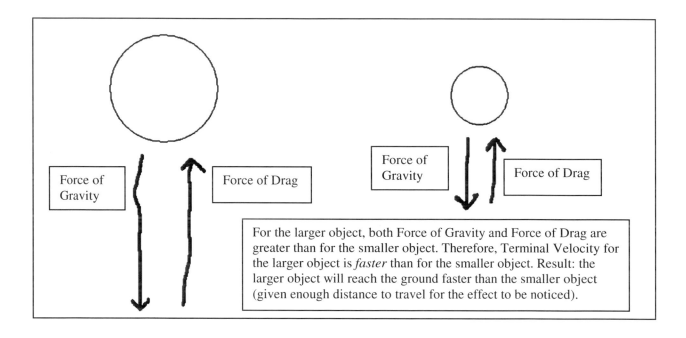

For the larger object, both Force of Gravity and Force of Drag are greater than for the smaller object. Therefore, Terminal Velocity for the larger object is *faster* than for the smaller object. Result: the larger object will reach the ground faster than the smaller object (given enough distance to travel for the effect to be noticed).

Chapter 9: Global Climate Systems

1. Benghazi, Libya, and Albuquerque, New Mexico both exhibit Steppe Climates, yet the cause of their dry conditions is quite different. Describe the primary factor responsible for the dry conditions at each location. *Bonus Question:* The precipitation recorded at Albuquerque is almost twice that recorded at Point Barrow, yet Albuquerque is considered a dry climate and Point Barrow a humid climate. Why?

A "Steppe" climate is found in semiarid regions where the available moisture is only enough to support the growth of short grasses with some shrubs. Steppe zones are typically found in the continental interiors of North America and Eurasia.

In order to answer this question, you *need to first look at a map* and find Benghazi, Libya, and Albuquerque, New Mexico. Benghazi, Libya is located on the Mediterranean coastline at 32° North Latitude, 22° East Longitude. Albuquerque, New Mexico is inland at 35° North Latitude, 107° West Longitude. Albuquerque's classification as a Steppe climate is easily understood; it is inland (relatively far from water) and is surrounded by a mountain zone to its west (thus creating a "rainshadow" effect). Benghazi, Libya is a bit more complicated due to the fact that it is close to the water (certainly, one would expect there to be more moisture available). What we find is that in Benghazi, the rate of evaporation is greater than the rate of precipitation; therefore it is a rather dry location (in other words, it doesn't rain much in Benghazi!). Notably, the rate of evaporation is quite high due to the fact that Benghazi is located within the movement of the Subtropical High pressure belt (which typically migrates between 30° and 33° Latitude dependent upon the season). The high pressure system continually forces air downward, in essence contracting the air and heating the atmosphere via "adiabatic" processes (see Question #7, Chapter 4). In addition, the water currents of the Mediterranean that flow near Benghazi tend to be cold, thereby decreasing the amount of moisture in the sky (remember, warm water will evaporate quicker than cold water. A warm water current, therefore, will provide a lot of moisture to the atmosphere which will eventually rain down).

Bonus Question: The precipitation recorded at Albuquerque, New Mexico is almost twice that recorded at Point Barrow, Alaska, yet Albuquerque is considered a dry climate and Point Barrow a humid climate. Why?

This question is all about relative humidity (see Questions #1, 2, and 3 of Chapter 5):

$$RH = \frac{(\text{actual water vapor } content \text{ in air})}{(\text{water vapor } capacity \text{ of the air})} \times 100$$

So, although the *actual* water vapor content in the air is higher in Albuquerque than it is in Point Barrow, the fact of the matter is that the *water vapor capacity* of the air in Albuquerque is also *much* higher than it is in Point Barrow. Therefore, the relative humidity in Albuquerque is lower.

2. Tropical B climates are located more poleward than A climates, yet their daytime high temperatures are often higher. Why?

The Koppen Climate Classification System reveals a strong latitudinal correlation between vegetation and climate. Although not exact, the following map can be used to approximate the latitudinal position of Koppen Climate zones:

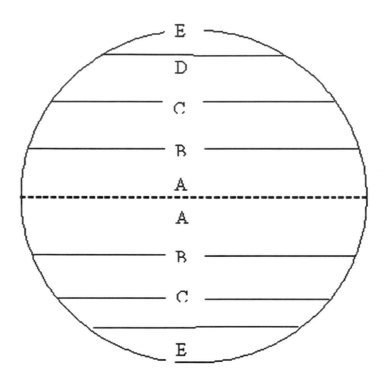

Notice that "A" climate zones are located on and around the Equator. This latitude is also home to the "Equatorial Low" pressure belt (or, the Intertropical Convergence Zone). Because this location is a low pressure zone there is a lot of cloud cover and a fair amount of precipitation (hence the reason that the rainforests are found here) – see Question #7, Chapter 4 and Question #2, Chapter 6. Cloud cover will block off some of the direct incoming solar radiation, thereby lowering the potentially high temperatures. "B" zones, on the other hand, are located on and around 30° North and South Latitude. Although B zones are more poleward than A zones, their daytime high temperatures tend to be higher. This is because the B zone latitude is also home the "Subtropical High" pressure belt. Due to the fact that this location is a high pressure zone, the sky is generally clear of clouds and is quite dry (hence the reason that deserts are found at this latitude). Because of this, solar radiation is not impeded as much as it moves through the atmosphere toward the ground (unlike the A zones). In other words, more direct solar rays strike the ground in the B zones than at A zones, making the B zones (typically) warmer locations.

3. Would you expect an area like Seattle, Washington to have a milder or a harsher winter than Grand Forks, North Dakota? What about summer? Explain.

For this question (as for the previous question) you *must first look at a map* and find the locations of both of the cities in question. You will note that both Seattle and Grand Forks are at almost the same latitude (47° North for Seattle, 48° North for Grand Forks). Therefore, climate differences due to latitudinal differences cannot be the answer. We also note that Seattle is located in the western United States (quite close to the Pacific Ocean) near a water way known as the Puget Sound. Grand Forks, on the other hand, is located inland. With this said, we would expect Seattle to have a milder winter than Grand Forks. Remember, water has a much higher specific heat than land (see Question #2, Chapter 6), therefore, although Seattle and Grand Forks are at the same latitude, the winter in Seattle is milder (i.e., not as cold and icy as Grand Forks) because the water keeps the atmospheric conditions slightly warmer. During the summer months, Seattle is actually cooler than Grand Forks. Just as the water moderated the temperature of Seattle during the winter, so does it moderate the temperature of Seattle during the summer. Summer months in Grand Forks are much hotter than summer months in Seattle.

4. How does vegetation in arid regions cope with lack of water?

Plants are highly adaptable and have evolved to their environmental surroundings. One knows this simply by looking at the apparent differences of a plant found in a tropical region versus a plant found in a desert region. The tropical plant tends to be greener, leaves thicker and larger, tissue more shiny than a plant found in a dry zone. Why is this? Plants are known as *autotrophs* or "self-feeders"; that is, they have the ability to convert solar energy into a chemical form. The process of converting solar energy into chemical energy is called *photosynthesis*. The resulting chemical energy is then used to feed the plant. *Respiration* is opposite to photosynthesis. When the plant uses the chemical energy to live, it is respiring (very similar to you or I taking in energy and oxygen). See the diagram below. During the photosynthetic process, the plant uses water (H_2O), carbon dioxide (CO_2), and solar energy to make carbohydrates (chemical energy). The reaction takes place on the green pigment of the plant known as *chlorophyll*. During photosynthesis, oxygen is released as a byproduct of the chemical reaction. During respiration, the plant uses the oxygen and the carbohydrates created during photosynthesis to feed itself. Respiration is the opposite of photosynthesis. During the respiration process, CO_2 is released as a byproduct of the chemical reaction (this is the same respiration process that all Earthly life goes through. For other creatures, however, carbohydrates are acquired by eating the carbohydrates not by converting solar energy into carbohydrates.).

In the photosynthesis and respiration processes, gases are exchanged from the atmosphere to the plant (and vice versa) via tiny pores on the plant leaf known as *stomata*. The size of the leaf (the *leaf area index*), therefore, is very important. For example, during respiration water is released back into the atmosphere via the stomata (*evapotranspiration*). See Question #8, Chapter 2. If a plant were unable to release moisture it would conceivably drown. If a plant released too much moisture it would conceivably desiccate and die. Therefore, plants with small leaf area reside in dry environments and plants with large leaf area reside in wet environments. In dry environments, the plant must hold onto moisture. If the plant leaf was too large, there would be too many stomata and the plant would lose too much water. In wet environments, on the other hand, the plant must release extra moisture. If the plant leaf was too small, there would be too few stomata and the plant would drown. By the way, the difference in the appearance of a plant due to its location is the foundation of the Koppen Climate Classification System.

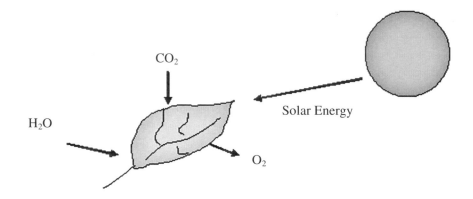

Photosynthesis: Solar Energy + H_2O + CO_2 = O_2 + Carbohydrates
Respiration: O_2 + Carbohydrates = energy (heat) + H_2O + CO_2

Dry environment plants are able to keep moisture in their tissue for a longer period of time. They are able to do this by a) having smaller leaf area, or b) by storing large quantities of moisture in their tissue (these types of plants are known as *succulents*).

Another adaptability that some desert plants have is the ability to photosynthesize at night! During the night, relative humidity is generally higher than during the day (see Question #1, Chapter 5), thus there is more moisture available for the photosynthetic process. These type of desert plants (known as "CAM" plants; *crassulacean acid metabolism*) store solar energy during the course of the day and then complete the photosynthetic process during the night!

There are other environmental coping mechanisms and adaptations. The key to this question and others like it is to remember that plants and animals generally look the way they do for a reason -- plants and animals will adapt due to the necessities of their surroundings.

5. In what way does the structure of a plant tell you about where the plant might exist?

See Question #4 above.

6. What color is the soil in the rainforest? What happens to the rainforest soil when the forest is cut-down? *Bonus Question:* Does the rainforest have nutrient-rich or nutrient poor soil?

This is one of those counter-intuitive questions. First of all, the answer to the first part of the question is not going to be as simple as "black" or "gray". It is a bit more involved. Ask yourself the following: *What happens a lot in the rainforest?* By definition, it *rains a lot* in the rainforest. The idea of lots-of-rain is going to be the key to this entire question.

Because it rains so much in the rainforest, lighter weight nutrients and minerals tend to get leached from the soil. What generally remain behind are heavier elements such as iron (by the way, this now answers the bonus question...the soil in the rainforest is *nutrient-poor*! Most of the nutrients get leached away with the rain. In addition, because there are so many plants that live in the rainforest, any available nutrient will get gobbled up quite quickly by existing plants. So, how do plants and animals survive if there are so little nutrients? The answer is a *very quick* nutrient cycle. As soon as nutrients fall from a tree – i.e., in the form of a falling leaf – it is turned almost immediately into mulch and purged back into the system!). Within rain are molecules of free oxygen. When this free oxygen encounters iron a chemical reaction takes place:

$$O_2 + Fe = FeO_2 = \text{iron oxide} = \text{rust!} = \text{red}$$

Now when the rainforest is cleared, the thick canopy that shades the ground is removed. So now it rains a lot and the ground has a tremendous amount of sunlight shinning on it. In essence, the ground begins to bake and the soil *laterizes*. Laterized soil is a hard-paned brick-like soil. Only extremely tolerant plants can grow on laterite. Therefore, the chopping down of the rainforest leads to a desolate, non-existent forest. This process is called *desertification* and is one of the major problems facing the rainforest today. Desertification not only affects the rainforest, but it affects global climate and weather too. How?

Chapter 10: Paleoclimatology

1. According to the climate record, how has climate changed over time? Are we presently in a cooling trend or a warming trend? Have humans aided in this trend? How so?

Interestingly enough, this is somewhat of a controversial political question. Is global warming due to humans or natural phenomenon? Many businesses (such as the oil industry) and many politicians (who cater to the oil industry!) would like to think that humans do not play a significant role in global climate. And, many "environmental" organizations (such as Green Peace) and many politicians (who cater to environmental organizations!) would say "yes", humans are the cause. Ultimately, science (without regard to money and politics) should be the guiding light. Let us first answer the question about global warming, then we will tackle the "human influence" question.

The following diagram depicts changes in global climate during the past 180 million years. Clearly, climate fluctuates over time, with both cooling and warming trends:

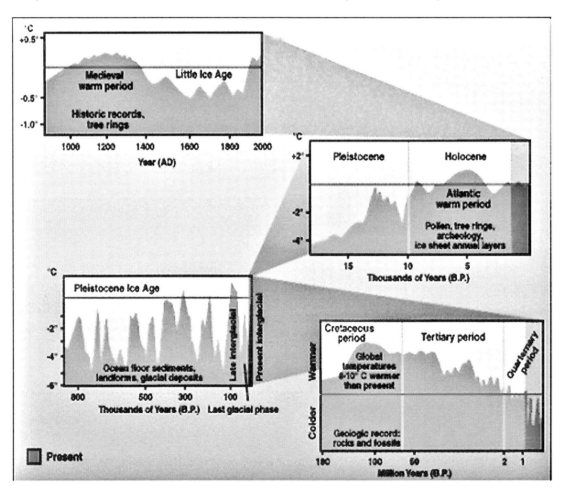

It is reasonable to note that 10,000 years ago, man was not on Earth driving cars and burning large amounts of fossil fuels. Therefore, we must concede that climate can change for reasons other than humanity. We can also see that we are presently living in a global warming trend. So, what are the causes of climate change and most importantly what are the causes for the worlds recent warming trend? Most researchers agree that this warming trend is in part due to human's burning of fossil fuels, deforestation, and the subsequent increase of atmospheric carbon dioxide (more on this below). Of course, human's dependency of fossil fuels (in large quantities) has only been occurring for the past century. Other variables to climate change include (but are not limited to):

- Volcanic Activity (producing ash in the atmosphere as well as outgassing of greenhouse gases such as carbon dioxide)
- Solar output (changes in the luminosity of the Sun)
- Milankovitch Cycle: Earth-Sun geometry changes (such as *eccentricity, obliquity, and precession*) – The figures below represent Earth as it orbits the Sun:

Eccentricity = 100,000 year cycle

Low Eccentricity   High Eccentricity

Obliquity

Earth's tilt changes from 21.5 to 24.5 degrees over a 41,000 year period

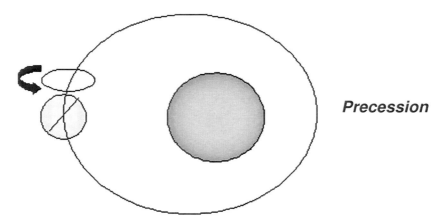

Precession

The Earth makes one complete "wobble" over a 23,000 year period

Okay, so climate can change for reasons other than human activities. But, what is the extent that humans play in the warming trend? The following graph indicates the *increase* in atmospheric carbon dioxide since the 1950's. Carbon dioxide is an important variable in warming processes due to the fact that carbon dioxide is a primary *greenhouse* gas (a gas that is able to absorb heat energy). Without carbon dioxide in the atmosphere, we would be a very *cold* planet. Of course, too much carbon dioxide means a very *hot* planet. Automobile exhaust and industrialization purges carbon dioxide into the atmosphere at a fast rate; much faster than the rate at which Earth is able to remove it from the atmosphere. Therefore, an imbalance is created and we find ourselves with too much carbon dioxide in the atmosphere. Hence, another potential reason for global warming:

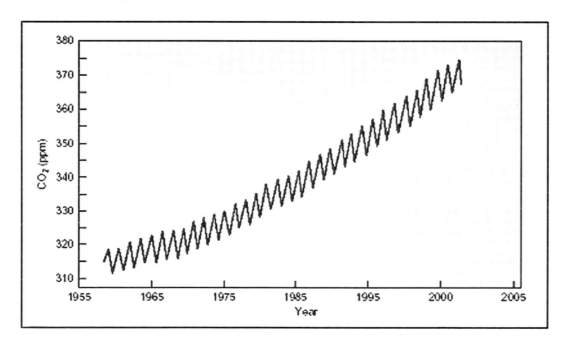

So now that we know there are both natural and man-made causes for climate change, which is more important? Now *this* is the question! What researcher's are finding is that the natural causes do not explain the extent to which climate is increasing. Therefore, humans are playing a role. Just how much of a role is still being studied. But let us be clear; global warming is not a fabrication. And global warming aided by human activity is not a fabrication either. By the way, global warming does not mean that it will be hot, hot, hot all the time. The nature of climate is to fluctuate from year to year and from season to season. Global warming could mean an increase in winter or summer temperatures of only 0.5 to 3°C. Even though this sounds like a very small amount, in truth it is very large to the global energy balance (over time, 0.5 to 3°C change would be enough to melt the ice caps and create incredibly unstable tropical weather conditions; i.e., more hurricanes, storms, and dynamic weather).

2. Researchers have suggested that global temperatures during the past century have increased by about 0.5°C to 1°C. They suggest that this trend will continue. Come on! Is a 1°C rise in temperature really that big of a deal? If it is, how so?

Yes! A 1°C rise in temperature (over time) could lead to the melt of ice caps and the creation of incredibly unstable tropical weather conditions. Remember, global warming does not mean that the temperature of Earth dramatically increase. Rather, it means that over time, the temperature of the Earth is steadily increasing (typically, during the winter months). If winter months increase in temperature by only a slight amount, that could be enough to lead to very "odd" conditions. Don't let the small numbers fool you. In this instance, a little means a lot!

3. What if the perihelion date changed from January 3 to June 10 and the other orbital parameters remained at present day values? How would this affect the intensity of the seasons *in each hemisphere*?

First, for a question like this you *must draw the picture!* Now, as you recall from Question #1, Chapter 2, *perihelion* is when the Earth is closest to the Sun, and *aphelion* is when the Earth is farthest from the Sun.

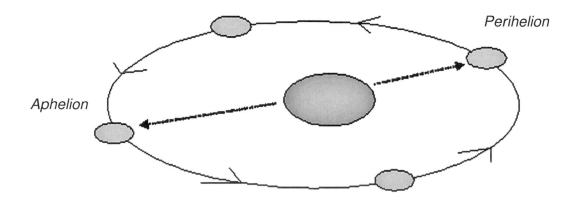

Coincidentally, perihelion (closest to) occurs during the northern hemisphere *winter*, and aphelion (farthest from) occurs during the northern hemisphere *summer*. Hence, the seasons are not due to the proximity of Earth to the Sun, but rather due to the Earth's tilt. However, does proximity play a role at all? What if we were to change the date of perihelion from the winter months to the summer months (i.e., what if we were *closest* to the Sun during the summer, not the farthest?) and what if we were to change the date of aphelion from the summer months to the winter months (i.e., what if we were *farthest* from the Sun during the winter, not the closest?), would the seasons be different?

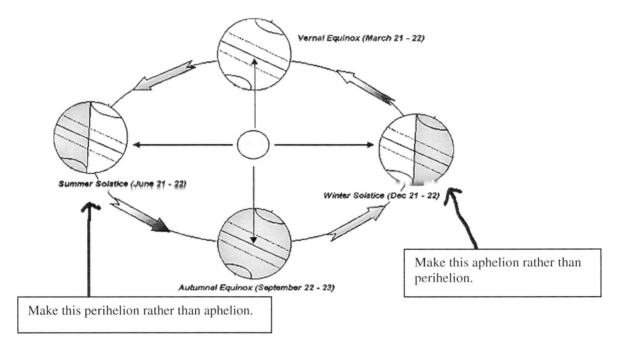

In a question such as this, your intuition needs to be your guide. Although the differences in perihelion and aphelion are minimal (about 2 million miles) that small distance is enough to provide slightly different amounts of solar radiation from reaching Earth. Therefore, if the seasons actually coincided with proximity (i.e., summer at the closest point and winter at the farthest point) we would most likely see slightly warmer summers and slightly cooler winters in the northern hemisphere. Now, the southern hemisphere would be a different story. Remember, the southern hemisphere seasons are opposite to the northern hemisphere seasons (when it is summer in the northern hemisphere, it is winter in the southern hemisphere. When it is winter in the northern hemisphere, it is summer in the southern hemisphere). Under present conditions in the southern hemisphere, perihelion actually coincides with summer, and aphelion coincides with winter! Although the southern hemisphere seasons, just like the northern hemisphere seasons, are due to Earth's tilt and *not* proximity to the Sun it is safe to suggest that changing the perihelion/aphelion dates would also affect the southern hemisphere: Winter in the southern hemisphere would be slightly *warmer* and summer in the southern hemisphere would be slightly *cooler* (although not by much...there is so much water in the southern hemisphere that slight changes in solar radiation would be subdued by the high specific heat of the ocean water).

4. How would a *decrease* in seasonality (i.e. warmer winters and cooler summers) lead to the advance of glacial ice on continents?

This is a rather simple question that need not be made difficult. During a typical year, glacial ice develops at high latitudes during the winter and then melts (or, recedes) during the summer. If we were to warm our winters (by 1 or 2° C) that would not be enough to stop the ice formation process found at high latitudes (where temperatures during the winter months fall well below the freezing point). On the other hand, if we were to cool the summer months (by 1 or 2° C) that would be enough to *slow* down the melt of ice. Ice would not recede as quickly during the summer. Hence, this could lead to the advance of glacial ice on continents. Ultimately, this could lead to an "ice-age". As noted in the questions above, little change means very large potential consequences.

Part 4: Dynamic Earth

Chapter 11: Rocks, Plate Tectonics, and Geologic Time
Chapter 12: The Oceans and Coastal Processes

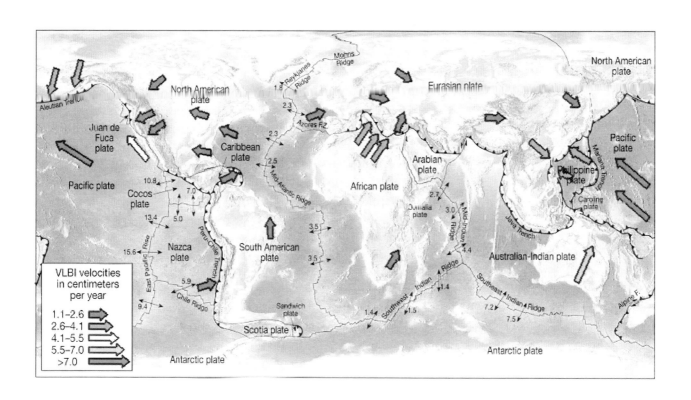

Chapter 11: Rocks, Plate Tectonics, and Geologic Time

1. Why does the Eastern U.S. have relatively little tectonic activity in comparison to the Western U.S.?

The world is like an onion, comprised of a series of layers (see Figure 1 below). Earth has a solid inner core, a liquid outer core, a mantle, and a crust. If we were to look closer, we would see that at the top of the mantle there is a plastic-like *asthenosphere,* and residing atop the asthenosphere is the solid *lithosphere* (comprised of the crust plus a thin portion of the upper mantle). The lithosphere is broken into about 14 big pieces known as *plates*. The motion of these plates atop the plastic-like asthenosphere is known as *plate tectonics*. As one plate moves, it collides with another plate (*convergence*), moves away from another plate (*divergence*), or moves side-by-side relative to another plate (*transform*) – see Figure 2. Figure 3 is a map showing the principle plates of the world, plate boundaries, and relative speeds and directions of plate motion.

Figure 1
Cross Section of Earth

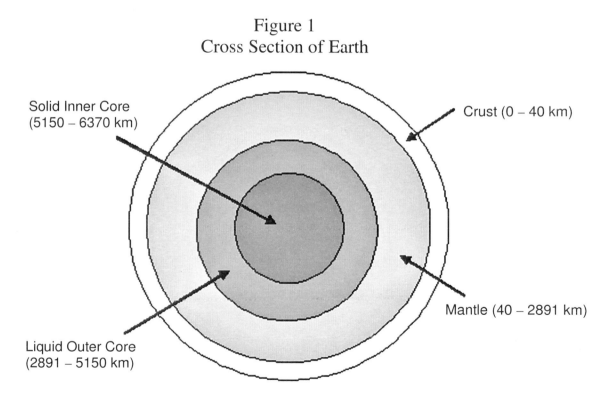

Solid Inner Core
(5150 – 6370 km)

Crust (0 – 40 km)

Mantle (40 – 2891 km)

Liquid Outer Core
(2891 – 5150 km)

Figure 2
Divergent, Convergent, and Transform (see Figure 3 below)

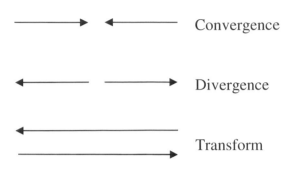

Figure 3
Plates, Plate Boundaries, and Relative Plate Velocity (in units of cm/year)

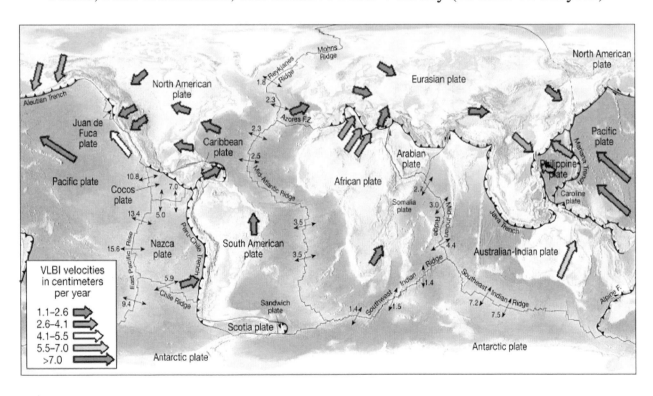

Plate tectonics has both "active" margins and "passive" margins. If you live along an active margin, then your location is very close to or on top of a convergent plate boundary. If you live along a passive margin, then your location is far from a plate boundary. In other words, the closer you are to a plate boundary, the closer you are to tectonic activity. As you can see from

Figure 3 above, western North American is adjacent to activity (active margin) whereas eastern North America is far from activity (passive margin).

2. Why is the Precambrian more difficult to decipher than more recent history?

Earth (and the Solar System) is about 4.6 billion years old. How do we ascertain what happened (geologically speaking) on Earth so many years ago? Certainly, 200 million years ago, there was no Scribe taking notes on what was happening to Earth. The way we decipher geologic history, therefore, is by looking at rocks (or, the *geologic record*). But what exactly are we looking for in the rocks? The key -- large in part -- is life; fossil evidence of years gone by. Fossil remains tell us something about past climates (as plant life is temperature sensitive), atmospheric conditions, geologic activity, and evolutionary processes. The study of past life is called *paleontology*. A paleontologist tries to solve the puzzle of Earth by sifting through layer after layer of rock and gazing into the fossil record – a window to our past. The fact finding mission of paleontologists has lead to the creation of the geologic time scale. The geologic time scale divides Earths history into a series of Eras, Periods, and Epochs based upon major transformations of life. Note the geologic time scale to the right. You will notice that 65 million years ago marked the end of the Mesozoic Era and the beginning of the Cenozoic Era. This boundary also marks the extinction of the dinosaurs and the advancement of mammals. Throughout Earth's history we note periods of extinctions and periods of advancements. The "why" and the "how" of the extinctions and advancements is the job of the physical scientist.

Take a close look at the geologic record. Note that the Precambrian dates from 4.6 billion years ago to 544 million years ago. 544 million years ago marks the beginning of the Paleozoic Era. You will also note that from 544 million years ago to today, geologic history is bound with layers of Periods and Epochs. This is in stark contrast to the Precambrian.

Era	Period	Epoch	Duration in millions of years	Millions of years ago
CENOZOIC	Quaternary	Holocene	0.01	0.01
		Pleistocene	1.8	1.8
		Pliocene	3.5	5.3
	Tertiary	Miocene	18.5	23.8
		Oligocene	9.9	33.7
		Eocene	21.1	54.8
		Paleocene	10.2	65
MESOZOIC		Cretaceous	79	144
		Jurassic	62	206
		Triassic	44	250
PALEOZOIC		Permian	36	286
	Carboniferous	Pennsylvanian	39	325
		Mississippian	35	360
		Devonian	50	410
		Silurian	30	440
		Ordovician	65	505
		Cambrian	39	544
PRECAMBRIAN				

Why? There are two reasons for this: 1) Fossil creation is difficult. In order for a fossil to be created, environmental and physical conditions need to be just right. If, for example, a bone is exposed to the atmosphere, it will weather away and eventually turn to dust. Therefore, a bone (or any other hard object) needs to be buried quickly in order to remove it from the atmosphere. The fact of the matter is, after so many millions and millions of years of existence on Earth, fossil remains from the Precambrian (if they did exist) could have eventually been exposed to the atmosphere and thereby weathered away. In addition, plate tectonics (see Question above) could have ultimately destroyed any existing fossil via the rock cycle. Or, 2) Perhaps we don't see many fossils during the Precambrian because there just were not many life forms during that time. Life began to flourish 544 million years ago. Prior to then, perhaps the atmospheric and environmental conditions were just not conducive to the development and advancement of life on our planet. Either way, the reason why we do not know too much about the Precambrian is, essentially, due to the fact that we have a lack of information (i.e., a sparse fossil record).

3. If the ages of Earth and the Moon are nearly identical, as believed, why are most rocks found on the moon so much older than Earth rocks?

The Moon has no atmosphere; the Earth does. The Moon has no plate tectonics; the Earth does (see Question #1 above). Rocks on Earth, therefore, undergo weathering and eventual "regurgitation" back into the Earth system via the rock cycle. Lunar (Moon) rocks do not. Therefore, any rock that is on the surface of the Moon today, most likely formed at the approximate time that the Moon was created. On Earth, however, those early rocks have long since been weathered away (into dust and sediment) and/or purged through the rock cycle. The oldest lunar rock that was collected during one of the trips to the Moon is about 4.4 billion years old. The oldest Earth rock (thus far found) is about 3.9 billion years old (found in Central Australia).

Bonus Question: Where are the oldest Earth Rocks located?

Answer: In the core of continents, such as in the central regions of Australia and Asia.

4. What is the best stone for a mausoleum: marble or granite? Why?

Granite. Marble is composed of calcium carbonate. When calcium carbonate is introduced to water it weathers quite quickly. In the "olden" days, many headstones were made with marble. Today, those headstones are nearly impossible to read (as the marble has been weathered). Granite, on the other hand, contains a molecule known as quartz. Quartz is incredibly resistant to weathering and will therefore last for a very long time.

5. What makes a volcano explosive versus more passive?

There are three major types of volcanoes: composite cone (also known as a *stratovolcano*), cinder cone, and shield volcano. A shield volcano tends to be less violent than either a cinder cone or a composite cone, and, composite cones tend to be the largest and most explosive of them all (the stuff of movies and myth). To understand why this is the case, we should look at a map of plate boundaries:

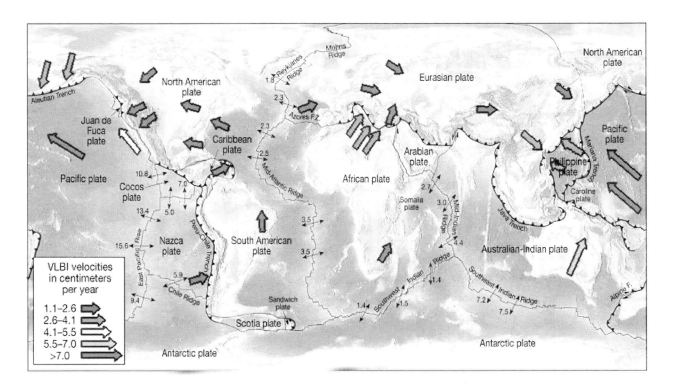

Hawaii is an example of a series of shield volcanoes. As a matter of fact, active volcanism is occurring on the Big Island of Hawaii today (a volcano known as *Kilauea).* Kilauea is a relatively tame volcano; that is, it erupts regularly, but the eruptions are not too explosive; lava spews out but not in a rage. Hawaii is located in the middle of the Pacific Ocean, far from any plate boundary. Compare Kilauea with Mount St. Helens (a composite cone volcano). When Mount St. Helens erupted in 1980, it was a violent explosion that blew off the top of the mountain. Mount St. Helens is located on the coast of the state of Washington, near the boundary of the Pacific Plate and the North American Plate. Clearly, location plays a large role in the type of volcano, but how does this location affect the explosive nature of a volcano?

Mount St. Helens is an example of a composite cone volcano; created by the collision of the Juan de Fuca Plate with the North American Plate. The collision has lead to *subduction*; Mount St. Helens (and the Cascade Mountain Range) is a result of the collision. The first image below shows the geographic locations of the Juan de Fuca Plate, the North American Plate, and the Cascade Mountain Range. The second image describes the collision.

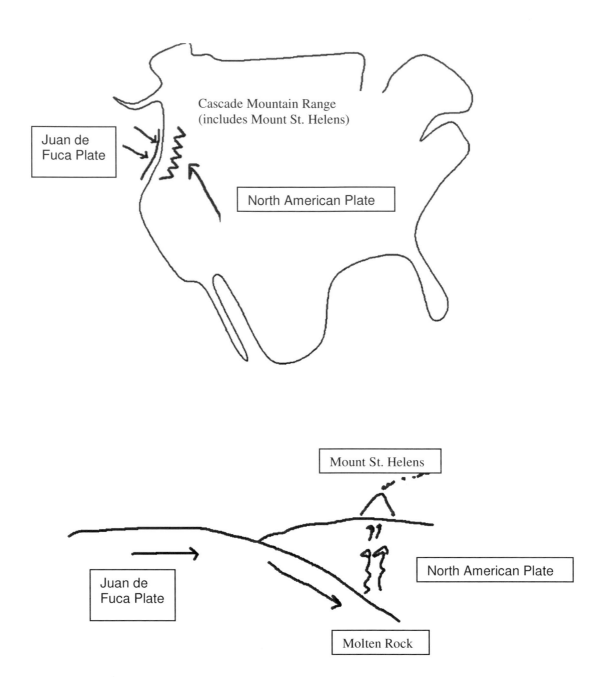

Notice in the second image describing the collision that the Juan de Fuca plate is subducted beneath the North American plate. Within the subduction zone (known as the Benioff Zone), there is a tremendous amount of heat and pressure build up. As a result, rock begins to melt and rise, inevitably becoming the beginnings of a volcano. The uniqueness of this type of volcano is the addition of quartz (silicon dioxide) into the melt via the surrounding continental rock. The North American plate is considered a *continental plate* due to the fact that it contains a large amount of continental rock. The Juan de Fuca plate is considered an *oceanic plate* due to its lack of continental rock. A major ingredient in continental rock is silicon dioxide (whenever you see the shimmer in beach sand, you are looking at silicon dioxide). Silicon dioxide is a long chain molecule; as such the molten rock thickens with the addition of silicon dioxide. Thick molten rock does not allow the easy escape of dissolved gases that are prevalent in the magma chamber. Therefore, *volatile* gases are able to build up to an explosive level. Eventually (and if there is no outgassing of the volatile gas), the rock structure of the volcano will not be able to withstand the energy build-up of the gas and will eventually pop. With regards to Mount St. Helens, silicon dioxide from the North American plate is added into the magma chamber. The addition of silicon dioxide thickens the magma, and creates the makings for a very explosive volcano. In other words, if you want to have an explosive volcano, be sure to have silicon dioxide as an active ingredient to your magma.

Imagine a bubble gum blowing contest. One contestant chews an *entire* pack of bubble gum, whereas the other contestant chews only one piece of gum. Of course, the first contestant is going to blow a *huge* bubble, and the second contestant is going to blow a small bubble. But when the bubbles burst, the guy who chewed the entire pack of gum is going to have gum in his hair and everywhere else. Imagine that silicon dioxide is gum and the hot air of the contestants breath is volatile gas. The more silicon dioxide there is, the greater amount of gas that is able to build up, and the greater the resultant explosion:

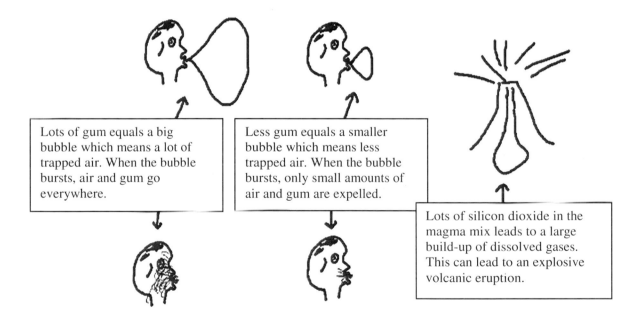

Lots of gum equals a big bubble which means a lot of trapped air. When the bubble bursts, air and gum go everywhere.

Less gum equals a smaller bubble which means less trapped air. When the bubble bursts, only small amounts of air and gum are expelled.

Lots of silicon dioxide in the magma mix leads to a large build-up of dissolved gases. This can lead to an explosive volcanic eruption.

6. How can we determine the location of an earthquake epicenter?

An earthquake is the result of plate movement and the subsequent collision of plates along plate boundaries. For example, when two plates collide frictional energy builds up (typically along the Benioff Zone -- see Question #5 above). In addition, when two plates move adjacent to one another (as is the case with a transform boundary – see Question #1 above), frictional energy builds up. When the frictional energy can no longer resist plate movement, the energy is released in the form of an earthquake. The point of this energy release is called the *focus*. The point above the focus on the surface of the Earth is called the *epicenter*:

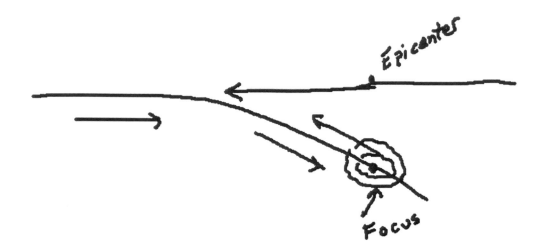

The energy emanating from the focus is in two distinct forms: P-waves and S-waves; both energy waves travel from the focus, outward. P-waves are *primary* waves. S-waves are *secondary* waves. In order to determine how far away the epicenter is from you, all you need to do is track the time difference of arrival of the P-wave and the S-wave at your location. In order to do this, you need to have a Richter Scale. The Richter Scale monitors P-waves and S-waves. If an earthquake occurs at some unknown location, both P-waves and S-waves will be traveling from its focus. The primary wave will reach your location first. Shortly thereafter the secondary wave will arrive. Because the P-wave travels consistently about 1.5 times faster than the S-wave, we can determine how far away the epicenter is simply by determining how much time the S-wave arrives *after* the P-wave. Perhaps a good analogy is a car race. Let us assume that there are two cars: car P and car S. Let us also assume that the top speed of car P is 100 mph and the top speed of car S is 50 mph. Assume that the cars start at the same starting point. After 1 hour of driving, car P is 50 miles ahead of car S (car P has gone a total of 100 miles and car S has gone a total of 50 miles). After 2 hours of driving, car P is now 100 miles ahead of car S (car P has gone 200 miles and car S has gone 100 miles). After 3 hours of driving, car P is now 150 miles ahead of car S (car P has gone 300 miles and car S has gone 150 miles). In other words, the longer car P and car S drive, the further ahead car P is of car S. This is what happens with our P and S waves. The further the epicenter is away, the greater the amount of time difference of arrival of the P and S waves.

Now, knowing the distance to an epicenter is nice, but *it does not* give us the location of the epicenter. For example, let us determine that an epicenter is 1000 miles away from us. Okay, but where is it located? We still don't know. We only know that the epicenter is 1000 miles away from us. In order to determine the exact location, we need to have at least three points of data. With three points of data, we will be able to *triangulate* the location of the epicenter:

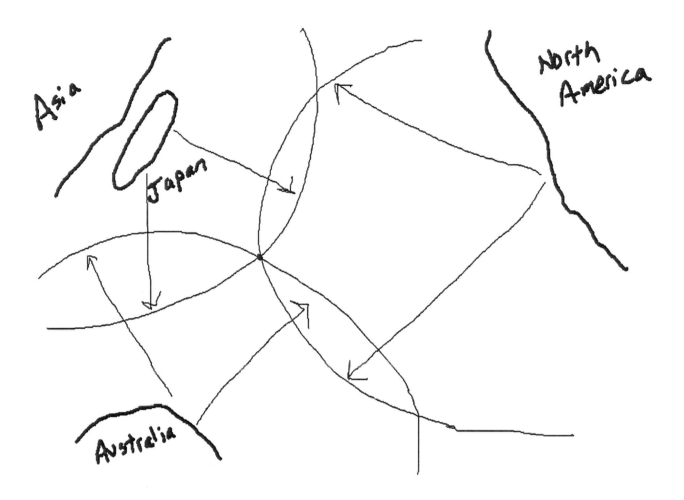

In the picture above, an earthquake has been detected by scientists in Japan (Tokyo), North America (Pasadena, CA), and Australia (Sydney). All three locations are able to determine how far away the epicenter is located from them. In order to determine the location of the epicenter, an arc is drawn from each location based upon how far away the epicenter is from that location. The point where the three arcs meet is the location of the epicenter.

7. What is the "Ring of Fire" and where is it located?

The Ring of Fire represents areas of high tectonic activity; where both earthquakes and volcanoes typically occur. Specifically, the Ring of Fire is the ring that surrounds the Pacific Rim (see Figure 3 below).

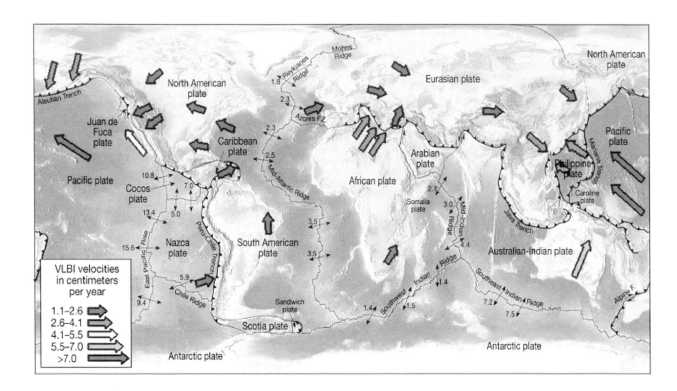

Figure 3
Plates, Plate Boundaries, and Relative Plate Velocity (in units of cm/year)

All along the Pacific rim (the imaginary boundary around the Pacific Ocean) there are active plate margins (see Question #1 above). Along these active margins are earthquakes and volcanoes; hence, the Ring of Fire.

Chapter 12: The Oceans and Coastal Processes

1. What is happening to the rotation of the Earth due to tidal frictional forces? So, what is happening to the length of day?

Fundamentally, the tide is a wave. The crest of the wave represents high tide and the trough of the wave represents low tide. Tides are so important to shipping that tidal records exist from nearly every harbor around the world for the last several *hundred* years.

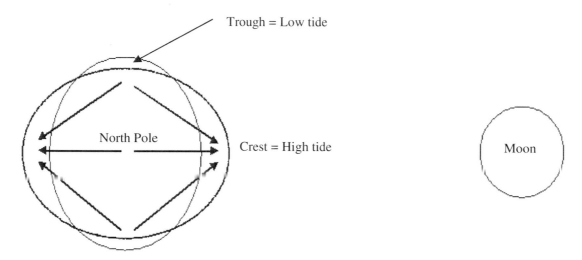

Gravitational Pull is toward the Moon. "Centrifugal" Pull is away from the Moon.
Result = 2 bulges on either side of Earth

Figure 1
Representation of High Tide and Low Tide
As Earth rotates, a location on Earth will rotate *into* high tide and *into* low tide.

Tides occur on Earth due to the gravitational pull of the Moon and (to a lesser extent) the Sun. In 300 B.C. a Greek philosopher named Pytheas observed the relationship between the phases of the Moon and the tides. But our understanding of tides wasn't fully understood until Newton in 1687 derived his gravitational force equations (see Figures 1 and 2) and Laplace in 1775 added to this with his Dynamic Theory of the tides.

Even though the Sun is much more massive than the Moon, we find that the Moon that has a greater effect on tides rather than the Sun. This can be explained by analyzing the Force of Gravity Equation. In the Equation, R is squared, therefore distance is more important than mass. Thus the Moon "wins" hands-down, as it is less than 200,000 miles away from Earth whereas the Sun is over 93 *million* miles away. Also note: Earth is solid, and therefore Earth bulging due to tidal gravity is quite small. However, when water and air are beneath the bulge, the gravitational pull can be quite high.

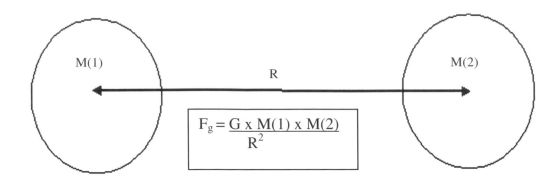

Figure 2
Force of Gravity between two Objects
M(1) is the mass of the first object, M(2) is the mass of the second object, G is the universal gravity constant, and R
is the distance between the two objects.

The Moon makes a complete orbit of the Earth in 29.5 days (a *lunar month*). The lunar month controls the tides (see Figure 1). During this time, the moon changes phases (see image below). The terms *spring* tide and *neap* tide are used to describe tidal conditions during a month. Spring tides occur twice a month (corresponding to New and Full Moon phases) and neap tides occur twice a month (corresponding to First and Third Quarter Moon phases). During spring tide, the Earth-Moon-Sun system is in alignment resulting in *constructive* interference of the lunar and solar tidal bulges (high tides are very high and low tides are extremely low). During neap tide, the Earth-Moon-Sun system makes a 90° angle resulting in *destructive* interference (high tides are lower and low tides are higher).

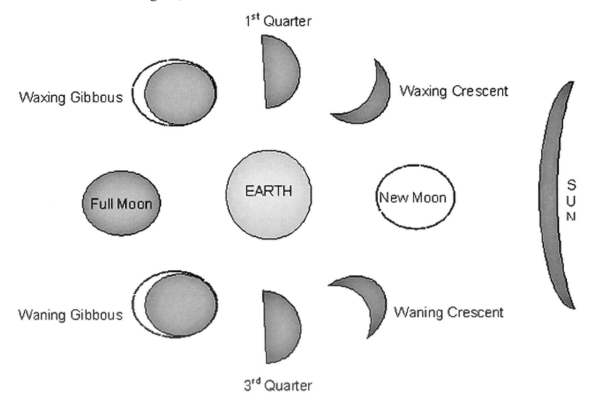

Standing on the shore, an observer sees that the tide comes in or goes out over several hours. But in reality the Earth's rotation is carrying the observer *into* and *out of* the tidal bulges. However, during the time that the observer is rotating on Earth, the Moon is also moving in its orbit around the Earth. That is why the *lunar day* (24 hours and 50 minutes) is slightly longer than the *solar day* (24 hours). It takes 50 extra minutes for the observer to be in the same exact position relative to the Moon after one rotation of the Earth. This explains why the Moon appears to rise about an hour later every night, and why the tides are almost an hour later every day…

Ultimately, tides are bulges created due to the gravitational pull of the Moon (and, to a lesser extent, the Sun). As you rotate into high tide, you are essentially rotating into the bulge. As you rotate into low tide, you are essentially rotating out of the bulge. These tidal bulges not only affect the height of the water but they also effect the rotation rate of Earth. The bulges create a frictional force that opposes Earth's rotation. Every time the Earth rotates into a bulge, the bulge acts as buffer, slowing down Earth's rotation. The extent of the slow down is quite minimal, but it exists nevertheless. A few million years ago, it only took about 23 hours for the Earth to rotate once on its axis. Now, it takes 23 hours and 56 minutes. As time goes on, Earth will continue to slow down and the days will continue to become longer until (eventually) Earth and the Moon will be locked in rotation. At the moment, only one face of the Moon is pointing toward Earth. This is due to the fact that it takes the Moon 29 days to both orbit one time around the Earth and to spin once on its axis. So, for an observer on Earth, we always see one side of the Moon. For an observer on the Moon looking at Earth, however, you will not see just one side of the Earth, but all sides. Earth is not locked with the Moon. It takes 24 hours for the Earth to spin once on its axis, and takes 29 days to for the Earth to rotate once around the Earth-Moon center of mass. Eventually (millions of years in the future), the spin and rotation rate of the Earth will be the same.

2. At which latitudes does seawater have the *lowest* salinity? What are some factors which cause this low salinity?

There are two major latitudinal locations where we find the lowest sea surface salinity. The first is at high latitudes during the summer time. During the summer, melting ice purges the sea with fresh water. The fresh water mixes with the sea water thereby lowering the surface salinity. At low latitudes (such as the equatorial region), there is so much rainfall due to the low pressure system, that fresh water is constantly being purged into the sea. Therefore, sea surface salinity at the equatorial regions tends to be lower as well. Where would one find areas of high sea surface salinity?

3. How do ocean waves change when they enter shallow coastal waters? What is the main factor causing this change in the waves?

One of the first things you notice while observing waves entering into shallow coastal waters is the "break" of the wave. Remember, a wave is horizontal moving energy. Although it appears that the *water* is moving horizontally, in truth, it is not. The diagram below depicts what is actually happening to the water as an energy wave passes through:

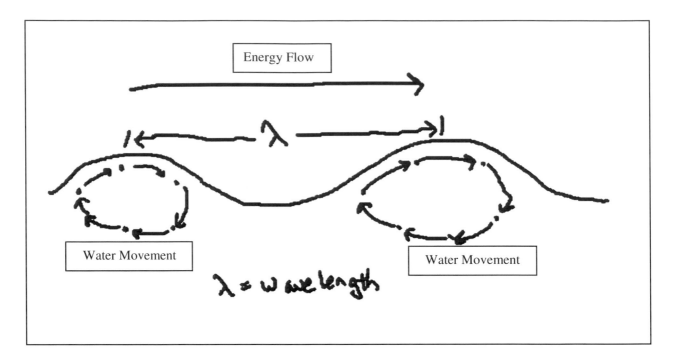

The water molecules are moving in a circular fashion. When the wave moves into an area of shallow water, the water moving up and down will begin to strike the bottom of the sea floor. When this occurs, the "brakes" are essentially pressed. Friction builds up and the bottom of the wave slows down versus the top of the wave. In addition, waves that are behind the slowing wave begin to push into the wave in front of it. The wave height begins to grow as the wave energy is squished together. Eventually, the ratio of wave height to wavelength will be 1:7. When this happens, the wave breaks.

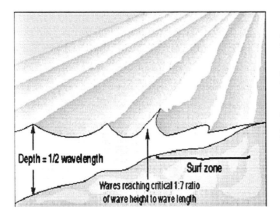

1. Wave approaches shore.
2. Water motion near bottom flattens, wave crests peak.
3. Bottom slows wave down, but waves behind continue at original rate. Wavelength is squished.
4. Wave approaches 1:7 ratio.
5. Water becomes shallower. Friction pulls bottom water. Crest moves forward, collapses. Break occurs at 3:4 ratio (wave height to water depth) = *surf.*

Appendix I

Measurements and Conversions

Time:

1 hour = 3600 seconds
1 day = 24 hours = 1440 minutes = 86,400 seconds
1 calendar year = 31,536,000 seconds = 525,600 minutes = 8760 hours = 365 days

Familiar Metric Approximations (from U.S. Metric Board Report):

Measurement	Metric Unit	Approximate Size
Length	Millimeter	Diameter of a paper clip wire
	Centimeter	A little more than the width of a paper clip wire
	Meter	A little longer than a yard
	Kilometer	Somewhat further than ½ mile
Mass	Gram	A little more than the mass of a paper clip
	Kilogram	A little more than 2 pounds
	Metric ton	A little more than a short ton (about 2200 pounds)
Volume	Milliliter	Five of them make a teaspoon
	Liter	A little larger than a quart
Pressure	Kilopascal	Atmospheric pressure is about 100 kilopascals

Temperature Formulas:

$$°C = (°F - 32) / 1.8 \qquad °F = (1.8 \times °C) + 32 \qquad Kelvin = °C + 273.2$$

Water boils at 212°F = 100°C; Water freezes at 32°F = 0°C
Body temperature = 98.6°F = 37°C
Absolute Zero = 0 Kelvin = -273.2°C

Metric to English Conversions:

Metric	Multiply by	to get English
Centimeters (cm)	0.3937	Inches (in)
Meters (m)	3.2808	Feet (ft)
Meters (m)	1.0936	Yards (yd)
Kilometers (km)	0.6214	Miles (mi)

Nautical mile	1.15	Statute mile
Grams (g)	0.03527	Ounces (oz)
Kilograms (kg)	2.2046	Pounds (lb)
Metric ton (tonne)	1.10	Short ton (US)
Meters/second (mps)	2.24	Miles/hour (mph)
Kilometers/hour (kmph)	0.62	Miles/hour (mph)
Knots (kn)	1.15	Miles/hour (mph)
Degrees Celsius (°C)	1.80 (then add 32)	Degrees Farenheit (°F)

English to Metric Conversions:

English	Multiply by	to get Metric
Inches	2.54	Centimeters
Feet	0.3048	Meters
Yards	0.9144	Meters
Miles	1.6094	Kilometers
Statute Mile	0.8684	Nautical Mile
Ounces	28.3495	Grams
Pounds	0.4536	Kilograms
Short ton (US)	0.91	Metric ton
Miles per hour	0.448	Meters per second
Miles per hour	1.6094	Kilometers per hour
Miles per hour	0.8684	Knots
Degrees Farenheit	0.556 (after subtracting 32)	Degrees Celsius

Appendix II

Blank World Maps

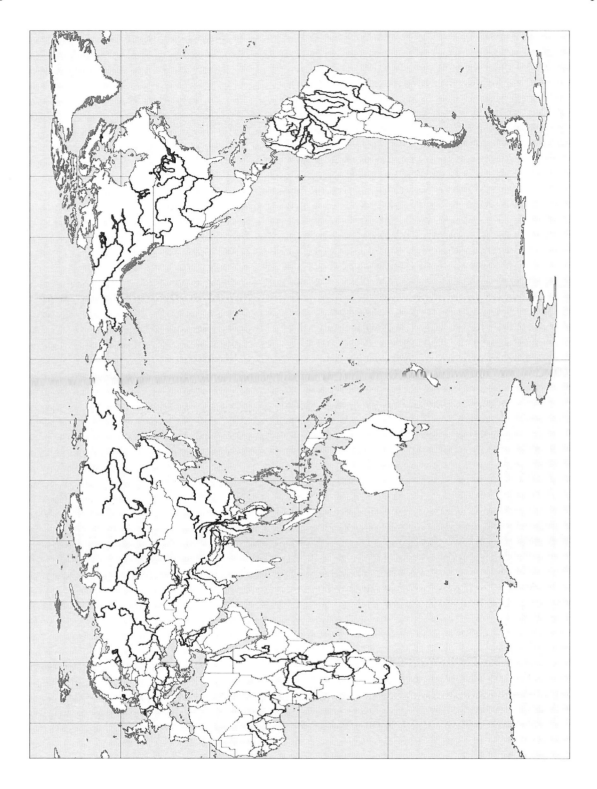

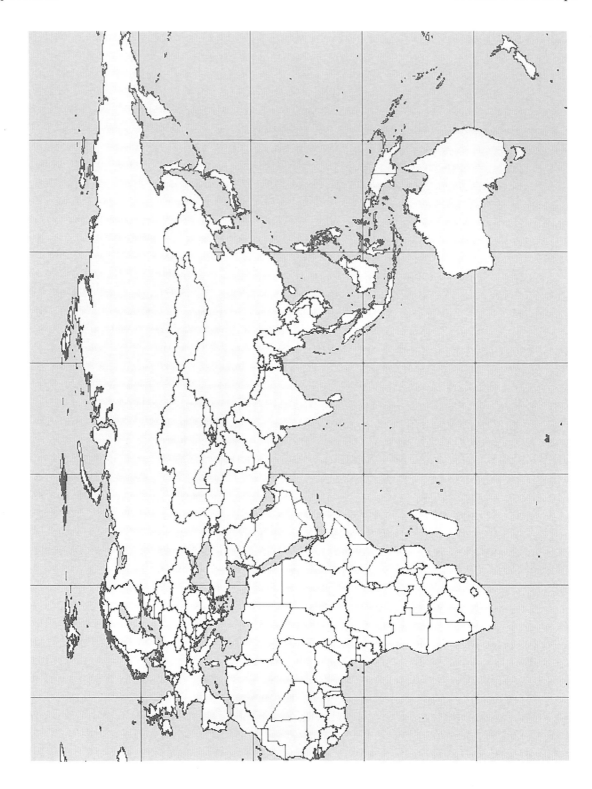

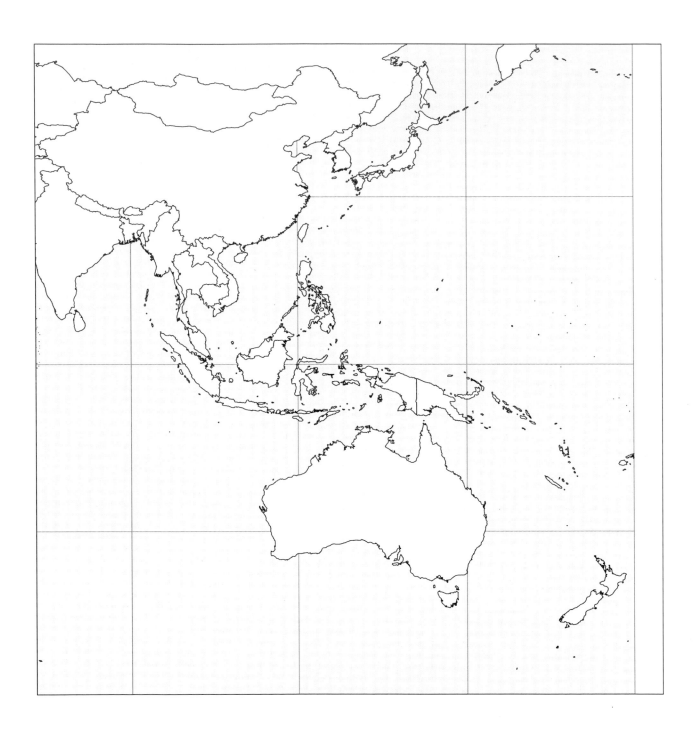

Appendix III

Rock Identification Tables

Igneous Rocks

		← ━━━━━ *ROCK NAME* ━━━━━ →		
Location of Crystallization	**Texture**	**Light Colored**	**Medium Colored**	**Dark Colored**
Intrusive (below ground) – Plutonic Rock	Coarse-grain	Granite	Diorite	Gabbro
Extrusive (above ground) – Volcanic Rock	Fine-grain	Rhyolite	Andesite	Basalt
	Glassy	Obsidian	Obsidian	Obsidian
	Vesicular	Vesicular Rhyolite	Vesicular Andesite	Vesicular Basalt
	Pyroclastic-fine	Pumice	Pumice	Pumice
	Pyroclastic-coarse	Contains large crystals (phenocrysts)	Contains large crystals (phenocrysts)	Contains large crystals (phenocrysts)

Sizes of Sediment

Sediment	Sediment Size (diameter)
Gravel	2 mm to 256 mm
Sand	1/16 mm to 2 mm
Silt	1/256 mm to 1/16 mm
Clay	< 1/256 mm

Clastic (Detrital) Sedimentary Rocks

Sediment Size	Composition	Features	Features
Gravel	Any	Concrete Look, rounded sediment	**Conglomerate**
Gravel	Any	Concrete Look, angular sediment	**Breccia**
Sand	Any	Cemented sand grains, any color	**Sandstone**
Silt	Any	Any color (can contain fossils). Layered	**Shale (siltstone)**
Clay	Clay minerals	Smooth feeling (can contain fossils). Layered	**Shale (mudstone)**

Biochemical Sedimentary Rocks

Any	CaCO₃ shells	Broken bits and pieces of shells cemented together. *Effervesent*	**Coquina**
Microscopic	Silicon dioxide skeletons	Smooth, silky feel; looks like chalk	**Diatomite**
Microscopic	CaCO₃ skeletons	Chalky color, gritty feel. *Effervescent*	**Chalk**

Chemical Sedimentary Rocks

Calcite ($CaCO_3$)	*Effervescent*. Calcite hardness. Usually light color. May have fossils.	**Limestone**
Silica	Hardness (7). White to gray (can be layered and colorful). May have fossils.	**Chert**
Carbon	Plant remains, black color, light weight. Will burn. Usually layered.	**Coal**
Gypsum (salt)	Hardness (2) = soft. White or light colored	**Gypsum**
Sodium Chloride (NaCL). Table salt	"Rock" salt. Cubes of salt bound together	**Halite**

Metamorphic Rocks

Rocks Commonly Derived From	Structure	Texture	Visible Minerals	Color	Other Features	Name	Grade
Shale	Foliate	Fine-grain		Variable	Flat, dull, breaks into smooth plates	Slate	Low
Shale	Foliate	Fine-grain	Mica	Variable	"Wavy" surfaces (breaks into plates)	Phyllite	Low
Shale, Siltstones, Basalts	Foliate	Coarse-grain	Mica, garnet, quartz	Variable	Mica conspicuous; finely foliated	Schist	Med
Usually Granite	Foliate	Coarse-grain	Feldspar, quartz, mica	Variable; white-gray	Banded, but foliation is visible. Breaks in blocks	Gneiss	High
Quartz, Sandstone, Chert	Non-Foliate	Medium-grain	Quartz	Variable	Interlocking grains. Breakage across grains	Quartzite	All
Limestone	Non-Foliate	Coarse-grain	Calcite	Variable	Crystalline masses; will *effervesce*	**Marble**	All

Index